PENGUIN PASSNOTES

WILLIAM SHAKESPEARE

# *A Midsummer Night's Dream*

STEPHEN COOTE, M.A., PH.D.

PENGUIN BOOKS

Penguin Books Ltd, Harmondsworth, Middlesex, England
Viking Penguin Inc., 40 West 23rd Street, New York, New York 10010, U.S.A.
Penguin Books Australia Ltd, Ringwood, Victoria, Australia
Penguin Books Canada Ltd, 2801 John Street, Markham, Ontario, Canada L3R 1B4
Penguin Books (N.Z.) Ltd, 182–190 Wairau Road, Auckland 10, New Zealand

First published 1986



Made and printed in Great Britain by
Richard Clay (The Chaucer Press) Ltd, Bungay, Suffolk
Filmset in 10/12 pt Monophoto Ehrhardt by
Northumberland Press Ltd, Gateshead



*The publishers are grateful to the following Examination Boards for
permission to reproduce questions from examination papers used in
individual titles in the Passnotes series:*

*Oxford and Cambridge Schools Examination Board, Southern Universities Joint Board.*

*The Examination Boards accept no responsibility for the
accuracy or method of working in any suggested answers given as models.*

# Contents

# To the Student

This book is designed to help you with your O-level, C.S.E. or G.C.S.E. English Literature examinations. It contains an introduction to the play, analysis of scenes and characters, and a commentary on some of the issues raised by the text. Line references are to the New Penguin Shakespeare, edited by Stanley Wells.

When you use this book, remember that it is no more than an aid to your study. It will help you to find passages quickly and perhaps give you some ideas for essays. But remember: *This book is not a substitute for reading the play, and it is your response and your knowledge that matter.* These are the things that the examiners are looking for, and they are also the things that will give you the most pleasure. Show your knowledge and appreciation to the examiner, and show them clearly.

# Introduction: Background to
# A Midsummer Night's Dream

A dream is a half-real, half-illusory experience in which fact and fantasy mingle. It is just so with Shakespeare's play. In it we are shown three groups of characters: the young and noble Athenian lovers, the 'rude mechanicals' or simple working men of the city, and those who inhabit the fairy world of Oberon and Titania. All three groups come to the wood and either contrive or undergo experiences which are sometimes beautiful, sometimes painful, but always magical. In each case, comedy and illusion combine. The young lovers quarrel and change their emotions under the influence of Oberon's power. Titania, the Queen of the Fairies, is made to fall in love with Bottom the weaver in revenge for refusing to hand Oberon a little Indian boy. Bottom, the great 'ham actor' among the mechanicals, is transformed into an ass and spends a magical night beside the Fairy Queen. Like the others, he eventually wakes to real life, unsure whether his experiences have actually happened or were just a fantasy. When the young lovers have also passed through illusions, been reconciled to Theseus, and so found happiness, they return to Athens in harmony, half remembering what has passed. Their enchantment is, to them, like a barely recalled dream. Finally, Titania wakes and finds her love for Oberon revived.

Back in Athens, the young lovers are married, and the occasion is celebrated by the performance of the mechanicals' play, a wonderful example of simple men trying to create a theatrical illusion and comically failing. And, at the close, the fairies also come to Athens. No longer are they the powerful forces who have so bewildered men in the wood. They are little sprites come to wish happiness to the mortals. When they have danced about the house, Puck – the most mischievous of them – steps forward and asks us to wake from the dreamlike world of the play by offering the actors our applause.

*A Midsummer Night's Dream* is both a play about magic and a magical experience. We must always think of its effect on the stage. If we do so, then we shall appreciate better the swift changes between farce and visionary loveliness, between suffering and delight. The language of the play is also rich and varied, and each of the three groups of characters has its own special poetry. Music sometimes helps to create the mood, while the visual spectacle should be truly beautiful.

*A Midsummer Night's Dream* is not an easy play. The language is fairly complex and you must use your notes to make sure you really know what it means. The plot, too, is difficult to remember. Indeed, it is sometimes as hard to recall as a dream itself. However, when all these problems have been mastered, the play remains a most engaging fantasy, full of poetry and delight.

# *Synopsis*

The play opens with the victorious Theseus expressing impatience to be married to his betrothed, Hippolyta, the Queen of the Amazons. Theseus, the Duke of Athens, has won her in a recent battle and their marriage will take place in four days' time. Theseus orders Philostrate to 'stir up' the young people of Athens and bid them celebrate his forthcoming marriage. The tone of happy revelry is interrupted by the arrival of Egeus, his daughter Hermia, and the two young men who are in love with her, Demetrius and Lysander. Egeus wishes Demetrius to marry Hermia but Lysander has 'bewitched' Hermia with his courtship. Egeus is deeply disapproving of this, and has brought the three young people before Theseus so that the Duke may impose the law of Athens. This states that Hermia must either marry the man her father has chosen for her or be executed. Theseus kindly and wisely tells Hermia that she should obey her father, but Hermia declares that her beloved Lysander is a worthy young man. In response to her request, Theseus explains that if she does not marry where her father wishes her to, then she must either die or live secluded for ever from the company of men. Hermia resolves to die or live as a nun rather than marry Demetrius, the man she cannot love. Theseus wisely suggests that she delay her decision until the time of his own marriage. In other words, Hermia has four days in which to make up her mind. Demetrius begs her to marry him, but his rival Lysander scornfully interposes and declares that he is quite as good a man as Demetrius. He then informs us that Demetrius has previously wooed a girl called Helena and then jilted her. Theseus remembers that this is indeed the case, and bids Demetrius and Egeus go along with him so that he can both give them some private advice and receive their help in preparing the festivities for his forthcoming marriage.

Lysander and Hermia – the two thwarted young lovers – are left alone on stage. They lament the position in which they find themselves and, while Hermia resolves to suffer in patience, Lysander declares he has a plan. Since the law of Athens forbids them to marry, they will run away from the city and live with an old aunt of his, safe from the Athenian law. Lysander suggests Hermia meet him in the wood outside Athens the following night. Hermia promises that she will do this, though her promise perhaps implies (see p. 27) that future events will not be quite so straightforward as they hope.

Helena – the young girl whom Demetrius wooed and then jilted – enters. She is still hopelessly in love with Demetrius and is suffering as a consequence of her feelings. She wishes she had Hermia's power to attract Demetrius's love. Hermia tells Helena that although she openly despises Demetrius, he none the less continues to love her. She then tells her to take comfort. She declares that she is going to flee from Athens with Lysander, the man she truly loves. Lysander tells Helena that they have vowed to meet up in the wood. Hermia adds that once they have indeed met, they will run away to a new life. Lysander and Hermia reconfirm their promise and then leave.

Helena is left alone on the stage and, in her soliloquy, reveals her unhappiness and tells us how love is blind, fickle and irresponsibly hasty. She thinks once again of her own feelings for Demetrius, and resolves that she will tell him of Hermia and Lysander's plan. This will ensure that Demetrius pursues them. Helena will then run after him. She will at least gain the benefit of seeing Demetrius in the wood. At this stage, she thinks she will then return easily from the wood to the city. Things will, of course, turn out very differently for her.

The second scene introduces us to the 'mechanicals', the ordinary working men of Athens, who have resolved to put on a play to celebrate Theseus's marriage. Peter Quince the carpenter is the director of the play, and his actors are Snug the joiner, Flute the bellows-mender, Snout the tinker, Starveling the tailor, and the wonderfully comic character of Bottom the weaver. The play that these simple men are to perform concerns the tragic story of Pyramus and Thisbe, two great lovers of antiquity. The tale of Pyramus and Thisbe is one of true love. It is a moving tale of two young people whose happiness is thwarted by their father. In this it bears obvious similarity to the plight of Lysander and Hermia. In the story of Pyramus and Thisbe, the lovers agree to meet not in a wood but at Ninus' tomb. When Thisbe arrives there she is mauled by a lion but she escapes. Pyramus finds her blood-stained garment and, thinking she is dead, stabs himself. Thisbe then returns to find the body of her lover and kills herself in turn. Bottom and his friends are quite incapable of presenting so heroic a theme, and we will laugh at their performance. None the less, we should notice how this famous tale of thwarted love is similar in several ways to the adventures of Lysander, Demetrius, Hermia and Helena.

As the mechanicals discuss their play, Bottom emerges as an over-keen actor who wishes to play all the parts in the tragedy. Young Flute resents playing the role of a girl. The slow-witted Snug is informed that he need not learn his lines. All he has to do is roar 'extempore'. The mechanicals are to create a dramatic illusion (see pp. 81–4). They are worried that this may be too realistic and so frighten their audience. They take ridiculous pains to make sure that this will not happen.

Act II introduces us to the magic world of Fairyland. Puck – or Robin Goodfellow, a figure from folklore – appears on stage. He talks to one of the fairies, and their language at once suggests the speed and wonder of the fairy world. Puck also informs us of a quarrel that has broken out between his master Oberon, the King of the Fairies, and his Queen. Titania has a little Indian boy in her care and Oberon wishes to have the child as his page. Titania, however, will not hand the boy over. Clearly all the fairies – including Puck – find the quarrels between the Queen and King fearful things. Puck then reveals to the fairy – and to us – that he is a mischievous spirit.

Oberon and Titania now enter. The quarrel which we have been told about is revealed to us in powerful language. Titania accuses Oberon of being unfaithful, while Oberon replies that Titania also has her favourites. Titania retorts that he is merely jealous, and then provides a vivid description of how the quarrel between Oberon and herself has led to terrible confusion in nature. Oberon declares that all could be made well if only Titania would hand over the little Indian boy. Titania says she will never do so. The boy's mother worshipped the Fairy Queen, but died giving birth to her son, and Titania has promised to rear the boy in gratitude for his dead mother's friendship.

Oberon has already informed us that he is devoted to the service of Hippolyta, just as Titania is the friend of Theseus. When Oberon now asks Titania how long she intends to stay in the wood, she declares that she will probably stay until after the time of Theseus's wedding. She then asks Oberon to join their 'moonlight revels'. If he does not wish to do so, he should leave her alone. Titania once more refuses to offer him the Indian boy and angrily departs.

Oberon is left alone with Puck. He vows to have his revenge on his wife. He summons Puck to him and describes how once when they were sitting on a promontory and listening to the music of a mermaid, Oberon saw Cupid, the god of love, fire an arrow at the heart of a royal virgin. Cupid's arrow missed its mark and fell on a flower which bled from the wound. The juice of this flower, when squeezed on the eyes of a man or woman, will make that person fall hopelessly in love with the next thing he or she sees. Oberon commands Puck to bring the flower to him. Puck exits, and Oberon declares that he will squeeze the juice of the flower on Titania's eyes. He hopes that when she wakes she will fall desperately in love with an animal passing by. When she has given him the Indian boy he will take the charm away with another herb.

Demetrius enters. He is being hotly pursued by Helena, the woman who loves him and whom he has jilted. He tells her roughly to leave him. Helena pathetically declares that she cannot do so, and that she is prepared to follow him like a spaniel. Demetrius becomes callous in his anger. He declares that the very sight of Helena makes him feel sick. He will run away and leave her to 'the mercy of wild beasts'. Clearly, some of these noble young lovers are nowhere near as noble or virtuous as we might have supposed them to be. Indeed, Demetrius runs off at this point, leaving his jilted girlfriend undefended in the wood. She declares that she will go after him. Oberon, who has made himself invisible while this angry dialogue has been taking place, now sees another opportunity to use the flower that Puck is bringing him. He promises that before these two lovers – Demetrius and Helena – leave the wood, the man will pursue the woman and the woman will flee from the man.

Puck enters and presents Oberon with the magic flower. Oberon then evokes with beautiful words the wild bank where it is Titania's habit to sleep. He divides the flower that Puck has brought him, takes part to squeeze on Titania's eyes, and presents the other portion to Puck, telling him to squeeze it on the eyes of a young man dressed in Athenian costume who is wandering round the wood and treating a young girl in a disgracefully heartless way. Neither Oberon nor Puck realizes that Demetrius is not the only young man in Athenian garments in the wood. Lysander is there too. Puck then leaves, declaring that he will do as Oberon has bid him.

The next scene is a delightful pageant which presents Titania being entertained by her singing fairy attendants. Their song lulls her to sleep and, once she is alone, Oberon enters and squeezes the juice of the flower on her eyes. He departs.

Lysander and Hermia – the true but thwarted lovers – then enter. They have lost their way. Indeed, they are so tired from wandering in confusion through the wood that they realize the only thing they can do is lie down and sleep till daybreak. There is an amusing exchange as Hermia begs Lysander not to lie quite so close beside her. When Hermia has got her way, the divided couple then fall asleep. Puck enters. He says that so far he has failed to find the young man in Athenian costume of whom Oberon has told him. No sooner has he said this, however, than he sees the separated Lysander and Hermia asleep on the ground. He naturally assumes that they have had a quarrel and that Lysander is the young man Oberon told him to find. Puck then dutifully – as he thinks – squeezes the juice of the magic flower on to Lysander's eyes. As soon as he leaves, Demetrius and Helena enter. The wretched young girl has caught up with the man who once wooed her but now despises her. Once again, he runs away and leaves her. Helena is exhausted and frightened. As she looks about her, she sees Lysander on the ground. She wonders if he is dead or only asleep and goes over to investigate. As she is shaking him, Lysander wakes up, sees her, and falls desperately in love with her. The juice of the flower has taken immediate effect. The unhappy and jilted Helena begs Lysander not to speak in the way he is doing. She thinks he is teasing her. Of course, neither of them realizes that Lysander is under the influence of the love potion Puck has squeezed on his eyes. In other words, neither Helena nor Lysander realizes that Lysander is a victim of an illusion (see pp. 81–5). None the less, the illusion is a very powerful one. Lysander declares that Hermia – the woman with whom he has run away – now means nothing to him. Helena is the most beautiful woman he can imagine. She, of course, again thinks that he is mocking her and also being quite exceptionally cruel. She rounds on him and tells him that such behaviour is not that of a true gentleman. She runs away to avoid him. Lysander, showing the combination of ardour and heartlessness with which we have seen the young men are characterized, leaves Hermia – the woman with whom only a few moments before he had been so passionately in love. He hopes he will never see her again. Helena now means everything to him, and he rushes off in pursuit of her. Left alone, Hermia wakes. She thinks she has been having a nightmare, but her very real fear becomes evident when she realizes she has been left alone in the middle of the forest at night. The hopes that she and Lysander shared of running away together and leading a happy life elsewhere now seem shattered.

The first scene of Act III returns us to the mechanicals and their play. These men have also decided to come into the wood. They think it is the safest place to rehearse. Quince tries to get the rehearsal started, but the over-eager Bottom declares that there are many things wrong with the play. For example, Pyramus will frighten the ladies drawing his sword, while the roaring of the lion will surely terrify them. He says that a prologue will have to be written which will tell them all that Pyramus does not really die and that the lion is only a disguised actor. It is significant that, while Bottom realizes that in putting on a play they are creating a dramatic illusion, he is also worried by the power of that illusion, and does his best to make sure that nobody is fooled by it (see pp. 81–6). Finally, the actors have to confront two technical problems. First, moonlight is necessary to their performance. They get a calendar and discover that the moon itself will indeed be shining on the night of their performance. Bottom declares rather imaginatively that they should leave open the window of the Great Chamber where they are to perform their play. Real moonlight will then pour in. Quince thinks he has a better idea. He will dress somebody up to appear like the man in the moon. In other words, they could have the real moon; instead they settle for a ridiculous illusion. Second, the tale of Pyramus and Thisbe requires a wall. Snout ludicrously comments that they could never bring a real wall into the Great Chamber. Bottom then solves this problem by suggesting that they dress somebody up as a wall and then get the actor to walk on stage. Nothing could be more ridiculous, and, when the mechanicals' tragedy is performed in the last act, much amusement will be derived from Snout's playing a walking, talking wall. Quince then tries to get the rehearsal going again while, unknown to him, the mischievous Puck enters. Puck is wildly amused by what he sees and hears. This is hardly surprising. Not only is it ridiculous that such characters as the mechanicals should play the parts of the great lovers of antiquity, they also get their roles hopelessly confused. They forget their cues or stumble over their words. But Puck has an even greater joke to play. When Bottom has retired behind a hawthorn hedge, Puck sticks an ass's head on him. When Bottom reappears – unaware that he has been transformed in this way – the horrified mechanicals run away. Bottom thinks that they are playing a trick on him, and he resolves to walk up and down and sing a song to show that he is not frightened. Bottom's song wakes the sleeping Titania. Again, the love juice takes immediate effect. The ravishingly beautiful Queen of the Fairies falls hopelessly in love with an ordinary Athenian working man who has been partially transformed into an ass. We are presented here with a wonderful combination of the beautiful and the funny. So hopelessly in love with Bottom has Titania become that she summons four of her little fairies to be his servants, and then promises Bottom all the pleasure he can imagine. We should note that the dialogue between Bottom and his four new fairy attendants is touching and tender.

At the opening of the second scene of Act I I I, Oberon wonders if Titania has woken up and fallen in love. Puck enters to tell him that Titania is in love with a 'monster'. He then tells Oberon about the rehearsal of the mechanicals' play, and of how he fixed an ass's head on Bottom. His mischievousness is made clear in the great pleasure he takes in telling how all the frightened mechanicals ran away and how Titania awoke to fall in love with the transformed Bottom. Oberon is delighted at the success of his plan, and then questions Puck as to whether he has squeezed the juice of the flower on to the eyes of the young Athenian. Puck tells him that he has.

Demetrius and Hermia enter. Demetrius is still, of course, passionately in love with Hermia, as he always has been. Indeed he has followed her into the wood, having been told by Helena of her plan to escape with Lysander. Hermia now violently rebukes him, not only because she does not love him but because she fears Lysander is dead and believes he is responsible. Lysander has, we know, abandoned his beloved Hermia in pursuit of Helena, the woman whom he now loves because of the love potion. Hermia chides Demetrius roundly and continues to do so despite his loving protestations. Eventually the angry Hermia runs away to seek out Lysander, leaving Demetrius, as he thinks, alone on the stage. He does not realize, as he declares that there is no point in pursuing Hermia any longer, that he is being watched by Oberon and Puck. Distressed and exhausted, Demetrius lies down to sleep.

Oberon is angry with Puck and the confusion that he has caused by squeezing the love potion on to the eyes of the wrong young Athenian. Puck seems to find the confusion amusing, but Oberon commands him to run through the wood and seek out Helena, while he squeezes the juice of the flower on Demetrius's eyes, hoping that when he wakes the first thing he will see is Helena, and that he will fall passionately in love with her once again. Puck leaves to do Oberon's bidding. The King of the Fairies squeezes the flower on to Demetrius's eyelids and Puck then re-enters, promising that Helena 'is here at hand'.

Helena enters pursued by Lysander, who is passionately in love with her as a result of the juice. Helena chides him for being unfaithful to Hermia, but Lysander declares that the love he feels for Helena is true. As Oberon has hoped, the noise of the quarrel between Lysander and Helena causes Demetrius to wake up. The magic potion at once takes effect. He sees the woman whom he once wooed and then jilted, and naturally falls passionately in love with her once more. Helena is now placed in an absurd and painful position: she is being pursued by Lysander whom she has never loved, while Demetrius, the man whom she cares for passionately and who has rejected her so cruelly, is now also talking to her like an inflamed lover. Far from being jilted and alone, Helena now has both the young men in the play making passionate advances to her. The position is a ridiculous one, but we should note that it is also truly painful to Helena, and her outburst makes this clear. Since she does not know that both Lysander and Demetrius are suffering from the illusion caused by the love potion, the only explanation that she can find for their sudden expressions of passion is that they have decided to gang up together and tease her. She thinks this is both very unkind and very ill-mannered of them. Needless to say, Lysander and Demetrius – now rivals for the once despised Helena's love – quarrel with each other. Lysander tells Demetrius that his true love is for Hermia, and that for him to court Helena is purely selfish. Lysander, who once possessed Hermia's love, now tells Demetrius that he can have her. Lysander surrenders all claims on Hermia. Demetrius rebukes Lysander.

As they quarrel, Hermia herself enters. Just as Demetrius treated Helena badly by jilting her before the start of the play, so Lysander – under the influence of the love juice – has treated Hermia badly. Not only has he jilted her, but he has abandoned her by night in the wild and dangerous wood. Indeed, as Hermia explains, the night is so dark that it is only the sound of Lysander's voice that has enabled her to find him. She asks him – naturally enough – why he has abandoned her. Lysander callously replies that there is no point in his staying by her when he loves another woman. Amazed, Hermia asks who this new love is. Lysander declares his passion for Helena, saying that she is more beautiful than the stars. Hermia quite simply cannot believe him. After all, they have eloped together. At this point Helena speaks again. Once more, the only interpretation she can find for the changes that appear to have taken place in the hearts of the three other lovers is that they have all of them conspired against her. So she believes that Hermia is part of the plot that has been hatched by the two young men to tease her in her wretchedness. Helena reminds Hermia of the happy times they spent together as girls. They loved and trusted each other like twins. Helena is appalled that Hermia should abuse their old friendship in this manner. Hermia is in turn equally amazed. Helena then suggests that Hermia has set her lover Lysander against her, and also persuaded Demetrius – the man she does not love, but who loves her – to act in the same way. Hermia is utterly bewildered by this attack, but Helena sees this as yet further proof of the plot she assumes they all have hatched against her. She vows to leave the other lovers, hinting that she may even be going to her death. Lysander passionately begs her to stay. Hermia begs Lysander not to tease Helena like this, while Helena merely scorns him. Demetrius then challenges Lysander, and the two young gentlemen bandy insults with each other. The confusion, the anger and the low language are all delightful. However, the effect of the threatened duel is to show Hermia how Lysander's feelings for her have apparently died. She now becomes convinced that he is truly in love with Helena. The callous young man declares that this is true and that he never wants to see Hermia again. She is furious. But, while she swears at him, Helena assumes that this is still part of the plot she thinks the others have contrived to tease her with. She calls Hermia 'puppet', and a marvellously comic argument breaks out between the two young women about their respective heights. Hermia thinks she is being taunted because she is short. Helena is terrified that Hermia will attack her. As she expresses her fears, she cannot help repeating the fact that Hermia is indeed shorter than she is. Lysander also teases her about her stature, and the two young men storm out, spoiling for a fight. Hermia and Helena, left alone – as they think – quarrel and part company.

When they have gone, Oberon and Puck step forward. Oberon is even angrier than he was before, while Puck – who is delighted by the complicated quarrel that they have just witnessed – declares that it is not his fault that he squeezed the love potion on the eyes of the wrong young man. He was told that he would identify him by his Athenian garments. As Puck says, it was not for him to know that there were two young men dressed in this way wandering in the forest. Oberon orders Puck to summon up a fog in which the quarrelling Lysander and Demetrius will get lost. Puck must then imitate the voices of the two young men and so bewilder and exhaust them that they will eventually lie down to sleep. When they have done so, Oberon will then take the charm off Lysander's eyes with the second herb, which he has already declared he will use on Titania when he has had his revenge. After this, Lysander will fall back in love with Hermia. The lovers will think that they have been involved in nothing more serious than a dream, and will return happily back to Athens and to marriage.

While Puck does as Oberon asks him, the King of the Fairies himself will seek out his wife, beg the Indian boy from her, and take the charm off her eyes. Puck says all this must be done quickly, as dawn is about to break. Evil spirits retreat before the light. Oberon makes it clear that he and his forces are not evil, and then departs.

Lysander enters and is confused by Puck's imitation of Demetrius's voice. Demetrius enters and is confused in his turn by Puck's imitation of Lysander's voice. Lysander re-enters, lies down and falls asleep. Puck then leads in Demetrius who also eventually falls asleep from exhaustion. Helena enters, tired from her attempts to fight her way back through the wood to Athens. She too lies down and falls asleep. Finally Hermia enters. She is drenched in dew and torn with briars. She has no more energy left. At last she too lies down to rest. When all four are safely asleep, Puck squeezes the antidote to the love potion on Lysander's eyes. So, when the lovers finally awake, Demetrius will still be in love with Helena because of the love potion squeezed on his eyes, while Lysander will fall back in love with Hermia because of the antidote that Puck has just applied.

At the beginning of Act IV, we move away from the world of the young lovers to that of Bottom and the Fairy Queen. We are shown the delightful pageant of Titania entertaining Bottom – whose tastes have become partly those of the ass into which he has been transformed – and then they fall asleep. Puck enters, and Oberon – who has been watching this scene – addresses him. He tells Puck how he found Titania wooing Bottom and how, so that she should be left alone with her new love, she surrendered to him the Indian boy. Having taken possession of this child – as well as the revenge he wanted on his wife – Oberon is now prepared to release Titania from the illusion that the love potion has caused. He also orders Puck to remove the ass's head from the sleeping Bottom. As Oberon squeezes the antidote on to Titania's eyes, she wakes and realizes with what she has fallen in love. Puck removes Bottom's ass's head to the sound of music, while the newly reconciled Fairy King and Fairy Queen dance together to express their revived love and the new harmony between them. Oberon declares that they too will join in the celebration of Theseus's wedding. The fairies then leave.

Dawn has broken. The fairy world has flitted away, and we are back in the world of the humans. Theseus's hunting party forms an excellent and noisy contrast to the dance of the fairies we have just witnessed. He and Hippolyta discuss dogs and hunting, and then glimpse the four lovers asleep on the ground. Egeus immediately recognizes each of them. He wonders why they are in the forest at all. Theseus suggests that they have risen early to observe the rites of May – the tradition by which young lovers went into the forest to gather flowers in the spring. He then bids his huntsmen wake them up with their horns. Lysander, the first to wake, immediately begs Theseus's pardon. After all, he had planned to run away from Theseus and the Athenian law with Hermia, despite her father's wishes. Lysander, half awake, explains this plot, and old Egeus interrupts him to demand justice. Demetrius then tells how he pursued Hermia – the woman he thought he loved – into the forest where, however, he found Helena and his old love reawakened. Demetrius – still under the spell of the love potion though he does not know this – declares that he only wishes to marry Helena now. Theseus wisely recognizes that the young people have found their true loves, overrules Egeus, and declares they will be married. With that he leaves. The four young people, left alone, can only interpret the experiences they have gone through as a dream. This is as Oberon had wished. They then return to Athens. Only Bottom is left on the stage. He too now wakes and, in a charming and moving prose soliloquy, tries to suggest something of the vision he has seen, declaring that he will get Peter Quince to write a ballad about it.

The other mechanicals are distressed by Bottom's absence. Their play cannot go on without him. They are sure he would have received a pension of sixpence a day if he had been available to play the part of Pyramus. As they bemoan his absence, Bottom enters and tells them the good news: their play has been chosen as the one that is to be performed before Theseus.

Act V opens with all three pairs of lovers – Theseus and Hippolyta, Lysander and Hermia, Demetrius and Helena – newly married. The story they have to tell of their night's adventures is a strange one. Theseus believes they have made much of it up, and extols the power of the imagination. Hippolyta believes that there is rather more to it than this, but she can provide no real explanation of what has happened. Theseus then asks for entertainment between supper and bedtime. Philostrate hands him a list of possible performances, and Theseus rejects them all in favour of the one which the mechanicals have prepared. Philostrate informs the court that the play is so ridiculous as not to be worth watching, but Theseus humanely declares that if it is performed in a spirit of love and loyalty then that is all he requires. He insists that this is the attitude that the court also take to the performance. But, during the ludicrous portrayal of the tragedy of Pyramus and Thisbe, all of the courtiers will make rather cruel remarks about the quality of the acting.

The play is a marvellous example of bathos – of grand intentions that appear ridiculous. Words and punctuation are ignored and the poetry is woefully inadequate. Starveling loses his patience with the audience, while all the actors contrive to destroy the dramatic illusion. None the less, this ludicrous performance gives Bottom – the great ham actor – a chance to show his talents. His lamentation and suicide as he plays the part of Pyramus are truly ridiculous. Once Pyramus and Thisbe are both dead, Bottom then starts up and asks the audience whether they would like an epilogue or a dance. Theseus tactfully suggests that a dance might be the most appropriate ending. Bottom and his fellows then perform a vigorous country jig. When it is over, midnight sounds and the lovers go off to bed. The stage is left to the fairies. Puck enters and offers a vivid description of the night. The King and Queen of Fairyland, bearing lights, then enter. It is a magical moment, made the more beautiful by the singing and dancing of the fairies. When this expression of magic and harmony is over, Oberon bids them all move through the house and rain blessings on the lovers.

Finally Puck is left on his own. He breaks the dramatic illusion and begs the audience to applaud if they have enjoyed the play.

# Scene by Scene Analysis

---

## ACT I SCENE i

The play opens with a speech from the victorious Theseus. He has just won a battle over the Amazons and is now to wed their Queen, Hippolyta. Theseus eagerly looks forward to the marriage. He declares that it will take place in four days' time but, like any true lover, he finds the delay irksome. Hippolyta tells him that the time will quickly pass and Theseus then orders his servant Philostrate to go and 'stir up the Athenian youth to merriments'. All of Athens will play its part in the celebrations surrounding Theseus's marriage. It is important to realize that marriage is seen in the play as something noble and joyous. It is also the state in which love finds its most mature expression. Theseus now turns to Hippolyta and declares that although he won her with his sword, he will wed her 'with pomp, with triumph, and with revelling'. Again, the note of joyful celebration that goes with marriage is sounded.

At this point Egeus enters. We should perhaps see him, in contrast to Theseus, as an older man. At once Egeus makes it clear that he is 'full of vexation'. He has promised his daughter Hermia in marriage to a young man called Demetrius. Hermia, however, is in love with Lysander. Egeus bids Lysander 'stand forth' and then proceeds to tell Theseus how this young man has 'bewitched' his child with his courtship. Lysander has sent Hermia poems, sung at her window by moonlight, and presented her with many little gifts. These, the old man believes, have 'filched' his daughter's heart. Lysander has won Hermia's emotions entirely. She no longer wishes to marry the man her father has chosen for her, and it is just this disobedience that Egeus finds distressing. He tells Theseus that he has come to claim 'the ancient privilege of Athens'. By this he means the harsh law which allows him, as a father, to marry his daughter where he wills or, if his daughter disagrees, to sentence her to death.

Theseus turns to Hermia. He recognizes that a daughter should obey her father. He also acknowledges that this Athenian law is a harsh one. Theseus informs Hermia that she should obey her father. He should be 'as a god' to her. He also assures her that Demetrius is 'a worthy gentleman'. Hermia bravely insists that Lysander is also a worthy gentleman, and she wishes that her father could see him as she does. She then asks Theseus to explain in detail how she will suffer under the law if she disobeys her father and refuses to marry Demetrius.

We may perhaps imagine Theseus at this moment summoning up his authority and looking compassionately at the young girl. He is the ruler of Athens and it is his responsibility to see that the law is obeyed. He tells Hermia that if she does not do as her father wishes, then she must either die or live out the rest of her life away from the company of men. Theseus recognizes that these are deeply painful options for the young girl, and he sensibly asks her to examine her feelings carefully. He wonders whether, if she refuses to obey Egeus, she really can live the life of a nun, 'chanting faint hymns to the cold fruitless moon'. Theseus sees that a life of chastity is a noble one, but he is also aware – he is, after all, himself a lover – that human love is a pressing need and something which promises great happiness. None the less, Hermia is adamant. She refuses to marry a man she does not love. The compassion of Theseus is again shown when he wisely suggests that any decision concerning Hermia's marriage be postponed until his own wedding day. In other words, Hermia has four days in which finally to make up her mind whether she will marry Demetrius as her father wishes, or face the cruel penalties of the Athenian law.

Demetrius interposes at this point. He is the young man whom Egeus wishes his daughter to marry. He is clearly in love with Hermia and he begs his rival Lysander to admit the justice of his case. After all, Demetrius has Egeus's consent, and it seems to him only just that the marriage should take place. Lysander replies scornfully. Since Egeus has so favoured Demetrius, Demetrius should perhaps marry *him*. Lysander knows that he himself is loved by Hermia. He believes it is his right to love the girl who responds to his own feelings. Egeus then rebukes Lysander, but the young man replies by saying that he is just as nobly born as Demetrius, that Hermia prefers him, and that he is quite as rich as – if not richer than – his rival. Again, he insists on the point that because Hermia truly loves him, they indeed ought to be married. Lysander now tells us something more about Demetrius. Hermia is not the first girl that Demetrius has fallen in love with. He has previously set about wooing young Helena, and she has clearly responded to his advances. Indeed, as Lysander makes clear, Helena is still passionately in love with Demetrius, despite the fact that he cruelly scorns her.

At this point Theseus speaks again. Lysander's words have reminded him that he already knows that the apparently virtuous Demetrius has been in love with another girl, the Helena whom he has jilted. Theseus claims that he was too busy with his own concerns to talk to Demetrius about this. However, he now orders the young man and Egeus to go and speak in private with him. As the ruler of Athens, he is going to give them some advice. He also turns to Hermia and offers more advice to her. He reminds her that it is her duty to obey her father, and if she does not then she will have to submit to the cruel penalties inflicted by Athenian law. Theseus declares that he cannot change these laws in any way. However, as we shall see at the end of the play, this is not quite the case. Theseus turns to Hippolyta, his future wife, and leaves the stage with her, Egeus and the young Demetrius.

Lysander and Hermia are now left alone on stage together. They are two young people in love and they see that the cruelty of fate is against them. As Lysander declares: 'the course of true love never did run smooth.'

We should look carefully at the language in which these two thwarted young lovers talk to each other. The language which they use is not realistic or natural; rather it is highly artificial and very beautiful poetry. The audience should respond to this. We may well be amused and touched by the circumstances in which they find themselves, but we should also appreciate the sheer beauty of the poetry they utter. For example, Lysander compares Hermia's cheeks to roses and asks why they are so pale. Hermia replies that they are fading for lack of rain, but she sees that her own tears could provide 'the tempest' to refresh them. The two thwarted lovers then show how true lovers are always crossed. Either, they say, the true lover falls in love with somebody of higher status, or with someone too young or too old. Lysander declares that even if love is returned, then 'war, death, or sickness' will thwart it. In a beautiful image – a picture conjured up in words – he sees true love as being like lightning. It is both very brilliant and very brief. Notice how his image of lightning is one of tremendous power. Through his words we come to see true love as a sudden and brilliant illumination that is swallowed up by 'the jaws of darkness'. We should be constantly attuned to language as beautiful and as powerful as this.

Since true love is so constantly thwarted, Hermia says that the only thing they can do is to be patient. Lysander appears to agree, but in fact he has a plan in mind. He tells Hermia that he has an aged aunt who lives seven leagues away from Athens. This aunt is childless, wealthy, and looks on Lysander as an only son. Lysander urges that they should run away and live with her. They will be safe in her home because it is far away from Athens and the cruel Athenian law does not apply there. He begs Hermia to steal away from her father's house the following night and meet him in the wood just outside Athens. This wood will, of course, play a crucial role in the *A Midsummer Night's Dream*. All the major characters will gather in it, and we should be prepared to see the wood both as a place of darkness and of danger, and as a place of magic and illusion. It is in the wood that love will be tested and true happiness eventually found. 'Wood', you may like to know, is an old word for 'mad'.

Hermia swears to Lysander that she will indeed do as he has suggested. But we should look carefully at the words she uses. She swears by both Cupid – who was the god of love and regarded as notoriously fickle – and by Dido, the Queen of Carthage, a faithful lover who was abandoned by her man. Perhaps these references help to suggest that once the lovers get into the wood, matters will not be quite as straightforward as they hope.

At this moment Helena enters. She is, we should recall, the girl whom Demetrius wooed before he turned his affections to Hermia. Helena is still passionately in love with Demetrius and makes this clear in her speech. She is deeply jealous of the fact that Hermia's beauty still attracts Demetrius. It seems so unfair. Helena wishes that she had the power and beauty to attract Demetrius in the way that Hermia can. She would give the whole world to have the influence over Demetrius that Hermia enjoys. How is it that Hermia is so powerful? Hermia says that she frowns at Demetrius, that she curses him, and that she hates him. This only makes Demetrius love her more strongly. However, Hermia bids the despised Helena take comfort. She declares that Demetrius will never see her again. She tells Helena that she is about to run away with Lysander. She can no longer bear to live in Athens where her love is constantly thwarted. Lysander then tells Helena that he and Hermia have resolved to steal away by night, and Hermia adds that they are going to meet up in the wood. Hermia provides us with a beautiful description of the wood as a place of flowers and of comfort, where she and Helena used to exchange girlhood confidences. She tells Helena that when they have met, they will fly away to a new world. She begs Helena to pray for them and wishes her well in her own pursuit of Demetrius. Begging Lysander to keep his word, Hermia then leaves. Lysander declares that he will indeed be faithful, and then bids adieu to Helena, who is left alone on stage.

Helena's soliloquy is an important speech. Again she expresses the pain of her unrewarded love. She cannot understand why she should be rejected. Helena feels that she is as beautiful as Hermia, but that this is irrelevant since Demetrius does not care for her. Demetrius is in the wrong, but she is also in the wrong for admiring Demetrius's qualities. After all, he has treated her disgracefully. Helena acknowledges, however, that love is not a rational or logical emotion. She shows this by describing the figure of Cupid, the god of love, to us. Cupid was usually painted as a blind and winged young boy. Helena declares that love is indeed blind like Cupid and that, like young boys, does not know how to discriminate between what is good and what is worthless.

In Helena's view, love is a fickle and inconstant emotion that makes worthless things seem admirable. The cruel Demetrius appears good to her only because she is in love with him. She knows that Demetrius is really as inconstant and fickle as love itself. She tells us so. None the less, she loves him; she has to. Indeed she loves him so much that she will go and tell him of Hermia's and Lysander's plan to run away with each other. She thinks that if she does this, Demetrius will pursue them into the wood. Helena will then follow him there, and will at least have an opportunity to see the man she loves.

The first scene introduces us to a number of themes which are crucial to *A Midsummer Night's Dream*. First, we see authority personified in the figure of Theseus. He tells us that marriage is a joyful and noble ceremony, the true and mature end of love. We also learn that love between young people is both very powerful and very fickle. The young people in this play seem to fall rapidly in and out of love with each other. As they do so, they experience great joy and also considerable suffering. At the end of this scene the plot is so contrived that all four young people will meet up in the wood outside Athens. Here love's qualities of fickleness, joy and suffering will be fully tested.

## ACT I SCENE ii

The young lovers are not the only ones who visit the wood; the comic characters in the play gather there too. The wood is where Quince the carpenter, Snug the joiner, Flute the bellows-mender, Snout the tinker, Starveling the tailor and the glorious figure of Bottom the weaver are going to rehearse a play. This is the play which they hope to be asked to perform in front of Duke Theseus as part of the celebrations of his marriage.

Quince the carpenter appears to be the director of the play. He asks if all the company are assembled. Bottom declares that he should read out the list of actors and tick off their names. Quince holds up the list of actors, but Bottom again interrupts to say that Quince should tell them what the play is about first, and then read out the names of the actors. It is made perfectly clear that Bottom is rather an over-enthusiastic character. It is also obvious that he easily gets involved in all sorts of contradictions. First, he asks Quince to read out the list of the actors, then, when Quince is about to do so, he asks him to tell the company what the play is about. Only when he has done this should Quince read out the list. The combination of enthusiasm and bungling will be important aspects of Bottom's character as it is developed.

Quince declares that their play concerns Pyramus and Thisbe. This was a famous story from classical literature, and many people in Shakespeare's audience would have known that it concerned thwarted lovers (see pp. 12–13). We may well remember the thwarted lovers that we glimpsed in the first scene. Bottom declares that the play is an excellent one and then once more bids Peter Quince read out the list of actors. Bottom's name comes first. He begs to know what part he is to play, and is told that he has been 'set down for Pyramus'. 'What is Pyramus?' he asks. Quince tells him that Pyramus is a 'lover that kills himself, most gallant, for love'. Bottom, the great ham actor, is enthralled by the possibilities with which this role will present him. He declares what a superb actor he will be, and yet the role that he would really like is that of 'a tyrant'. Bottom is the sort of ham actor who likes nothing more than to rant and rave on the stage. He gives the assembled company a ludicrously awful example of how he would set about this.

The other characters are now told what their roles will be. Young Flute is given the part of Thisbe. He hopes that this will be a romantic one; he would like to think that Thisbe is 'a wandering knight'. Quince tells him that Thisbe is Pyramus' lover. Flute is horrified at the thought of having to play a woman. 'I have a beard coming', he claims, rather pathetically. Bottom immediately speaks up. Not only does he want to play the part of Pyramus, he also wants to play Thisbe, and proceeds to show the assembled company how he would do this. Quince patiently informs him that he must play the part of Pyramus only. Quince then tells Starveling the tailor that he must play Thisbe's mother, and informs Snout that he must play the part of Pyramus' father. The slow-witted Snug speaks up. He asks if the lion's part has been written yet. He is, he declares, 'slow of study'. He will need as much time as possible to learn his role. Quince tells him there is no need for him to learn his words. He can improvise his role, 'for it is nothing but roaring'. Needless to say, such a role appeals enormously to Bottom, who wants to play the lion as well. He boasts that he will do it so well that the Duke will ask him to roar again. The character of this over-enthusiastic ham actor is once again made clear. Peter Quince declares that if Bottom were to perform the part of the lion as he says he would, then he would frighten all the ladies in the court 'and that were enough to hang us all'. The assembled company of actors agree. Bottom's ludicrous reply is that he would roar in a gentle way, 'I will roar you an 'twere any nightingale.' Quince, perhaps rather impatient by now, tells Bottom that he can only play the part of Pyramus. Bottom accepts this but he then asks what sort of beard he should wear. Quince says that he can wear whatever sort of beard he likes. The scene ends with Quince begging all the actors to learn their roles and meet again in the wood outside the city. If they rehearse their play in the city, everyone will know what it is all about.

This is a delightful comic scene. The ordinary men of Athens have got together to put on a play to celebrate their Duke's wedding. Their loyalty is very touching. It is also very amusing. It is ridiculous that such people should try and stage a tragedy. Their dramatic ambitions are made all the more absurd by their having Bottom in their company. We cannot fail to laugh at such a man, and the thought of him playing a tragic hero is charmingly silly. However, the idea that these men should put on a play at all, that they should try to create an illusion, is a very important one in the play. This aspect of *A Midsummer Night's Dream* is discussed more fully on pp. 81–6.

## ACT II SCENE i

We have met the aristocratic lovers in the play, we have also met the low–life characters who are going to provide much of the comedy. We now meet Puck and we see the world of the fairies and the magic that provides so much of the play's appeal.

Notice the swift effortless verse of the fairy who speaks to Puck. We immediately sense a world of lightness, speed and magically transformed nature. The fairy is the servant of Titania, the Fairy Queen, and he provides us with a description of her world of flowers and natural beauty. We get a suggestion that Titania is a powerful force in the natural world.

However, just as things are unsettled in the world of the mortal lovers, so there is trouble in the world of the fairies. Puck is the servant of Oberon, the King of the Fairies, and he informs us that there is strife between Oberon and Titania. Oberon is 'passing fell and wrath' because Titania has in her possession a boy stolen from an Indian king. Oberon is 'jealous'. He wishes to have the child for himself. Titania will not give him to her husband, however. Instead, she surrounds the child with flowers 'and makes him all her joy'. The result is great dissension. Titania and Oberon can never meet without an argument, and so terrible are the exchanges between them that all their attendant elves 'creep into acorn cups and hide them there'. We are given the impression once again that Titania and Oberon are both powerful forces in the natural world, which is important. Both the Fairy Queen and the Fairy King do indeed enjoy great power. We will see that they have enormous influence over the behaviour of human beings when they are in the forest. But we should also recognize that when, at the end of the play, we return to the human world, these fairy forces are diminished to little, benevolent spirits.

Realizing who he is, the unnamed fairy turns to Puck and identifies him as that mischievous spirit known also as Robin Goodfellow who is constantly causing problems. It is Puck who is responsible when things go wrong in the household. If the milk cannot be churned into butter, it is Puck's fault. If people get lost at night, it is because Puck has misled them. (Indeed, later in the play, Puck will cause Lysander and Demetrius to get lost.) This element of sheer mischief in Puck's character is of the greatest importance, and Puck now proceeds to boast about his power. He sees it as his role to make Oberon laugh. He does so by disguising himself as a horse, or transforming himself into a crab-apple and so frightening old ladies that they fall off their stools. The relish of Puck's language here makes us aware of his enthusiastic and irresponsible nature. He is a figure of fun, a source of confusion. As such, he has a strong influence on the plot.

Oberon and Titania enter from opposite sides of the stage. It is a marvellous moment in the theatre, and if we are only reading the play we should try our best to imagine its effect. Both Oberon and Titania will be magnificently dressed, surrounded by their fairy servants. They appear as a beautiful and powerful King and Queen. The power of the language with which they scorn each other can then be truly appreciated.

We have already been told by Puck of the dissension between Oberon and Titania. Now it is made clear to us. 'Ill met by moonlight, proud Titania!' is Oberon's greeting. Titania bids her fairies fly away and, detained by Oberon, rounds on him for his infidelities. Oberon, King of the Fairies, has the power to change his shape. He has disguised himself as Corin, a shepherd, and wooed young country girls such as the 'amorous Phillida'. She then declares that the only reason Oberon is in the wood at all is because his mistress Hippolyta is about to be married to Theseus. He has come 'to give their bed joy and prosperity'.

Titania is obviously jealous of the relationship between Oberon and Hippolyta. Oberon rounds on Titania in his turn. Has not Titania favoured Theseus? Has she not saved him from peril when Theseus was courting other women? Titania declares that Oberon is merely jealous. What he says are 'the forgeries of jealousy'. She is referring partly, of course, to Oberon's jealousy about the little Indian child that Titania has in her train. She goes on to show the effects that such jealousy and wrangling have had. What she says provides us with a powerful picture of the influence she and Oberon have in the natural world. Because there is strife between them, the natural world is in confusion. Since the King and Queen of Fairyland no longer meet in harmony, nature has turned wild and confused. Sea fogs are falling on the land, the rivers are overflowing, nothing grows, the wheat has rotted, the sheep are refusing to breed, the countryside has become a waste land, disease is everywhere, and the seasons have become confused.

Oberon answers with scorn. If nature is in confusion, it is her fault and she can set things to rights. All she has to do is hand the little Indian boy over to Oberon. Titania refuses to do so: not the whole wealth of Fairyland could buy him from her. She then explains why. The boy's mother worshipped Titania and the two women spent many happy hours gossipping with each other as they watched the great trading ships crossing and recrossing the ocean. Just as the sails of the trading ships grew bigger in the wind, so the Indian princess became 'big-bellied' with her child. However, the princess died in the course of giving birth, and Titania has vowed to bring him up in memory of her.

Oberon tartly asks Titania how long she intends to stay in the wood. She declares that she will probably be there till after Theseus's wedding day. She then asks Oberon to join in her revelry. If he will not, then he should leave her alone and she will ignore him. Oberon once again begs Titania to give him the boy. If she does so, then he will happily take part in the Fairy Queen's revels. Titania refuses Oberon's request and, sensing that a serious argument will break out if she stays any longer, she orders her fairy train away.

Oberon is angry and contemptuous. He wants his revenge. He declares that Titania will not leave the wood until he has tormented her for the discomfort she has caused him. Oberon summons Puck to his side. He bids Puck remember how they once sat upon a promontory and heard a mermaid that was riding on the back of a dolphin and singing the most rapturously beautiful songs. Puck says that he remembers the occasion. Oberon then tells him that while they were enjoying this beautiful spectacle, Oberon saw Cupid 'all armed'. Puck could not see the god of love, but Oberon was aware of how Cupid drew his bow and shot an arrow at the heart of 'a fair vestal thronèd by the west'. It is generally reckoned that this is an allusion to Elizabeth I, who was famed for her virginity. When Cupid fired his arrow at anybody's heart, it was believed that they would fall in love. However, on this occasion the arrow missed its mark,

> *And the imperial votaress passed on*
> *In maiden meditation, fancy-free.*
> (ll. 163–4)

Though the arrow did not land where Cupid intended, 'it fell upon a little western flower'. The flower was once milk-white but when the arrow fell on it; it bled, and it is now 'purple with love's wound'. Oberon orders Puck to go and fetch the flower. He declares that the juice of it, once laid on the eyelids of a sleeping man or woman, will make that person fall passionately in love with 'the next live creature that it sees'. Oberon bids Puck bring the flower to him instantly. Puck does as he is told, declaring that he can encircle the earth in forty minutes. Once again, the speed, lightness and grace of the magical world of the fairies are emphasized.

Oberon is left on his own, and his soliloquy informs the audience what he intends to do. Once Puck has provided him with the magic flower, he will squeeze its juice on the eyelids of the sleeping Titania, so that the minute she awakes she will fall in love with the first live thing she sees, regardless of what it is. Perhaps Titania will fall in love with a wild animal. Oberon evidently hopes she will be humiliated in some such way. He then informs us that he can remove this charm when he wants by applying to Titania's eyelids the juice of another herb. Oberon clearly intends to have his revenge, and to amuse himself. None the less, the fact that he has an antidote to the flower which Puck has been sent to gather is important. The illusion Oberon will inflict on Titania will not be permanent. This information will have a great bearing on the rest of the plot of the play.

Now Demetrius and Helena enter. Helena has informed Demetrius that Lysander and Hermia have vowed to meet in the forest before running off together. Just as Helena knew he would, Demetrius has pursued the two lovers. He wishes to keep Hermia for himself. Demetrius now turns on Helena, the woman he no longer loves. He tells her bluntly that he hates her, and then asks where Lysander and Hermia are. He vows that he will slay Lysander. The fact that he cannot find his Hermia is driving him mad, he declares. Again he tells Helena to go away. Helena pathetically replies that she cannot leave him. Her love is so strong that she is bound to follow him. Demetrius cruelly tells her that she has no reason to love him and that he cannot love her. As Helena declares, this only makes her love him the more. She sees herself behaving like his dog. So strong are her feelings that she does not mind the humiliation which is inflicted on her. Demetrius tells her that her behaviour is both absurd and dangerous. To follow him into the wood at night in this way is ridiculous. Helena says that she believes she is quite safe because Demetrius is a virtuous man. In fact, as we have already seen, he is behaving in a callous and shallow way at this moment. Indeed, he threatens now to run away and leave Helena 'to the mercy of wild beasts'. Eventually he does go, and the desperate Helena runs off in pursuit of him.

The whole episode has been watched by Oberon who has been both amused and rather touched by it. He promises that he will turn the tables: before the two young lovers leave the wood, the girl will fly from the man and the man will pursue the girl. It is just this sense of irresponsible fun that both Oberon and Puck enjoy.

At this moment Puck returns with the promised flower and gives it to Oberon. There follows a fine speech. Oberon declares that he knows the place in the forest where Titania holds her revels and in the end goes to sleep. His description of this place is of the greatest beauty (see p. 78). Oberon conjures up for us the richness of nature and the sheer delight of the fairy world. He will drop the juice of the flower that Puck has brought him in Titania's eyes 'and make her full of hateful fantasies'. Oberon bids Puck take some of the juice. He tells him that an attractive young Athenian lady is in the wood. She is obviously hopelessly in love with a young man who despises her. Oberon bids Puck drop the juice of the flower in the young man's eyes, so that when he awakes he will fall passionately in love with the girl. Oberon tells Puck he will recognize the young man 'by the Athenian garments he hath on'. What Oberon obviously does not realize is that there is another young Athenian man in the woods – Lysander. Puck will get the two confused.

## ACT II SCENE ii

The revels of the Fairy Queen commence. Here we must imagine the effect on stage. We should both picture the visual beauty of the scene – Titania surrounded by her attendant fairies – and use our ears to listen to the words and the music that the fairies sing. We should have the impression of the most delightful fantasy as the song of the fairies lulls their Queen to sleep.

When Titania has fallen asleep, Oberon enters. He has in his hand the flower that Puck has brought him. He walks over to his sleeping wife and squeezes the juice of it on her eyes, wishing as he does so that when she wakes she will fall in love with some wild animal. His hope is that she will 'wake when some vile thing is near!' Oberon leaves.

Lysander and Hermia now enter. They have met up in the wood as they arranged but, of course, they have got lost. As Lysander admits rather futilely: 'I have forgot our way.' He sees that the only thing that they can do is rest until daylight. Hermia agrees, and says that she will lie down on a nearby bank. Lysander begs to lie beside her but Hermia, rather amusingly, fends him off. Lysander claims his intentions are entirely innocent, but Hermia charmingly replies that she does not believe him. Again, she begs him to observe 'human modesty' and lie a little way from her. Lysander reluctantly agrees. They then lie down apart from each other and very soon fall asleep.

No sooner are they sleeping than Puck enters. He has been all the way through the forest but cannot find the Athenian about whom Oberon has told him. Now he glimpses Lysander on the ground and immediately mistakes him for Demetrius. After all, the sleeping young man is wearing 'weeds of Athens'. The young man whom Oberon sent him to find would be dressed, Puck was told, in exactly the same way. Puck's suspicions that he has found the right young man are confirmed when he sees Hermia lying a little way off from Lysander. He naturally assumes that they have had a quarrel. Relieved that he has found the man he was sent to seek, Puck squeezes the juice of the flower on Lysander's eyes and sets off to report back to Oberon.

Helena and Demetrius enter: Helena is still doggedly following the man she loves; Demetrius is still roughly trying to shrug her off. Eventually he runs away without her and Helena is left, as she thinks, on her own. In her soliloquy she once more wonders what power Hermia has that she is so attractive to Demetrius. It seems to her that she is 'as ugly as a bear' by contrast. After all, Demetrius has fled from her. And then she sees Lysander asleep on the ground. She is concerned. Is Lysander dead or asleep? She can see no blood, and so she shakes Lysander to try and wake him up. Lysander stirs, opens his eyes and, of course, falls for the first creature that he sees. He is passionately in love with Helena. He declares that he will run through fire for her sake, that she is the most beautiful woman in the world. He wonders where Demetrius is and vows that he will run the young man through for treating Helena in the way he has. The confusion is delightfully ridiculous.

Helena tries to calm Lysander down, and tells him that he should be happy because he is here in the forest with Hermia, the woman who loves him. He should be content.

Lysander pours scorn on such an idea. Under the influence of the love juice, he repents every tedious minute he has spent with Hermia. He ironically declares that his reason, his logical intelligence, can now see that Helena is infinitely more attractive than Hermia. He is unaware he is suffering an illusion (see pp. 81–6) and thinks that his taste has now matured and that he can appreciate Helena's real worth. These are the words of a truly impassioned lover. Neither Lysander nor Helena knows that Puck has squeezed the juice of the flower on his eyes and that, as a result, he is acting under an illusion. Indeed, this sudden change in Lysander's behaviour can only be interpreted by Helena as a form of cruel mockery. Is it not enough, she asks, that Demetrius scorns her? Must Lysander be cruel to her as well? The young man is treating her in a disgraceful way. She bids him farewell. She sadly confesses that she thought Lysander was more of a gentleman than he appears to be. She is appalled that he should be so apparently cruel as to mock a woman who is suffering from hopeless love. With this, Helena runs away.

Lysander vows to pursue her. The power of his illusory love is immense. He looks at Hermia, and now she makes him feel as sick as he would if he had eaten too many things. He bids Hermia lie where she is and vows to leave her in the forest. Passionately and ludicrously in love with Helena, Lysander rushes off in her pursuit.

Hermia is left on the stage, alone and asleep. She is having a nightmare. She thinks that a snake is crawling over her and eating her heart away, while Lysander looks on smiling. As she wakes up, she looks round for Lysander. Of course, he has gone. Hermia is on her own in the middle of the forest. She is terrified, and vows to run off and either find Lysander or die.

## ACT III SCENE i

Bottom and his friends are also in the wood, which is, according to Quince, 'a marvellous convenient place for our rehearsal'. With a true director's eye he at once sees how one area can serve for their stage, while the hawthorn hedges can be their 'tiring-house' or green-room, the place where the actors can rest when they are not acting.

Bottom, however, foresees problems with the play. He sees 'things in this comedy of Pyramus and Thisbe that will never please'. For example, Pyramus has to draw his sword and kill himself. The ladies of the court will not be able to abide this. Snout agrees with him, and Starveling suggests that they 'must leave the killing out'. They cannot understand that a play is only an illusion (see pp. 81–6). It is a 'make-believe', like the illusions of the young lovers which we have already seen.

This problem has clearly bothered Bottom, and he believes he has found a way out of it. Rather than asking the audience to enjoy the illusion that the actors will present, Bottom says that a prologue should be written in which the actors can announce that they 'will do no harm with our swords, and that Pyramus is not killed indeed; and for the more better assurance, tell them that I, Pyramus, am not Pyramus, but

Bottom the weaver. This will put them out of fear.' What Bottom does not realize is that the prologue will destroy the dramatic illusion which he and his friends are trying to create. None the less, Quince agrees that they should have such a prologue. Snout then wonders if the ladies won't be frightened of the lion as well. Starveling is sure they will be. Bottom thinks that they must do something about this. What he suggests is that half the actor's face should be visible through his costume. It will then be obvious that the lion is not a real one. Further, Snug the joiner, who is to play the part of the lion, must tell them not to be frightened. He is not really a lion. He is Snug the joiner, acting out the part. Quince agrees to this. But, good director that he is, he sees two further problems. Pyramus and Thisbe must meet by moonlight, and he wonders how this can be arranged. Bottom asks if the moon will actually be shining on the night of the performance and, when he finds out that it will be, he suggests intelligently that they leave open the window of the room where they are to present their play. They will then have real moonshine. Quince suggests a far more ridiculous solution to the problem: they can have one of their company play the part of Moonshine. He obviously thinks that this will be far more convincing than the real thing. Quince's second problem is that the story has Pyramus and Thisbe talking to each other through a wall. Clearly they must bring a wall into the Great Chamber where they are to perform their play. Snout is appalled by the problems that this will cause: 'You can never bring in a wall.' The solution is obvious to the inventive Bottom. Someone must pretend to be a wall. An actor will have to come on stage covered in plaster, loam or roughcast to suggest that he is a wall. He will then have to hold two of his fingers apart to suggest the cranny through which Pyramus and Thisbe can whisper to each other. The mechanicals now believe that they have solved all the problems of putting on their play, and they settle down to rehearse.

Puck enters, and is amused by the antics that he sees. He realizes that they will provide him with a splendid opportunity to do some mischief.

Quince summons his leading actor on stage. This is Bottom's great opportunity. He strides out – and gets his words wrong. Having corrected himself, Bottom completes his ludicrous speech and exits. Puck is as amused by the absurdity of all this as we are in the audience, and he follows Bottom off stage. Flute, who is not sure of his cue, eventually comes forward. If we are only reading the play, we should imagine the comical effect as this ridiculous young man dressed up as a girl, utters his flat and ridiculous lines. He manages to get these wrong. Quince, no doubt rather impatient by now, corrects him. He then realizes what has happened: Flute has delivered all of his lines in one speech. 'You speak all your part at once, cues and all.' The harassed director now tries to get the rehearsal going once more. But Bottom forgets *his* cue and Quince has to call him on stage. His appearance is one of the most wonderfully comic moments of the play. While Bottom has been in the 'tiring-house' behind the hawthorn hedge, Puck has placed an ass's head on him. Bottom does not realize this, of course, but when he appears on the stage – looking like an ass – the mechanicals are terrified and rush away. Puck chases them, delighting in the mischief he has caused.

Bottom has no idea what is happening. He asks why they have all run away. Then he thinks he understands. His friends are playing a trick on him to make him frightened. As Puck chases the mechanicals, we should perhaps imagine them peering round the corners of the stage and glimpsing the transformed Bottom. They cannot believe what they see.

Bottom is now convinced that he has seen through their cruel trick. He thinks his friends are trying to 'make an ass' of him. He has not the faintest idea that he does actually look like an ass. He resolves to be brave and defiant. Rather touchingly, he declares: 'I will walk up and down here, and I will sing, that they shall hear I am not afraid.' Bottom opens his mouth to sing the promised song. Perhaps we should imagine it coming out of his ass's head as a mixture of braying and human speech. However that may be, the noise of Bottom singing is enough to wake the Fairy Queen. Titania is roused from her 'flowery bed' and listens, enraptured by what she hears. She has, as Oberon had hoped, fallen in love with the first thing she has seen – a very ordinary man of Athens, disguised as an ass. Just as Lysander, when he woke, fell suddenly and desperately in love with the wrong person, so Titania lavishes all her affection on the ridiculous figure before her. Nothing could be more absurd. But we should see that we are required to do far more than laugh here. Certainly, what we are looking at is ridiculous, but we should also realize that it has great poetry and pathos about it. While we laugh we should bear in mind that the very ordinary and down-to-earth Bottom, though humiliated by Puck, has none the less won the love of the magically beautiful Titania. It is not the aristocrats, the great people in the play, who will be presented with the most profoundly engaging experience. It is Bottom the weaver who will spend the night with the Fairy Queen.

She begs him to continue with his song. She tells him it is very beautiful, and adds that she has fallen in love with his own beauty. She sees this ordinary Athenian, transformed as he is into an ass, as the very personification of all that is most attractive. She declares again that she loves him.

A fine comic actor will be able to portray the amazement that must sweep over Bottom at this point; he will also be able to bring out the pathos of Bottom's very ordinary reply when he is told by the Fairy Queen that she is passionately in love with him. For the moment, all he seems to want is to get out of the wood. Titania says that he will not leave. She will hold him there by magic if necessary. She begs Bottom to go with her, and creates for him a most delightful picture (ll. 148–52) of the life that he will lead in her company. She then summons four attendant fairies: Peaseblossom, Cobweb, Moth and Mustardseed. She tells them to attend Bottom and to provide him with anything that he wants. Once again, Titania's speech reflects the lovely fairyland world of nature. The four attendant fairies now greet Bottom, and the gentleness with which he speaks to them is both charming and touching. Once he has made the acquaintance of each of them, Titania leads her new-found lover away to her bower.

## ACT III SCENE ii

Oberon reappears. He is wondering if Titania has woken yet and, if she has, what she has fallen in love with. Puck enters. Oberon asks him what has been happening, and Puck replies: 'My mistress with a monster is in love.' He describes the mechanicals' play, ridiculing the rehearsal and thoroughly enjoying his account of how he broke it up when he placed the ass's head on Bottom. With great energy he tells how he chased the other actors away, leaving Bottom alone, and how Titania awoke and fell in love with an ass. Oberon is delighted. Such humiliation inflicted on Titania is better revenge than he could possibly have hoped for. He then asks Puck if he has squeezed the juice on 'the Athenian's eyes'. Puck proudly claims that he has done that as well.

Demetrius and Hermia now enter. Demetrius, as we know, is passionately in love with Hermia. It soon becomes obvious to Puck and Oberon that Puck has made a dreadful mistake. The magic potion has been squeezed into the eyes of the wrong young Athenian. Demetrius protests his undying love while Hermia scorns him. She is suspicious that Demetrius may even have slain her beloved Lysander. Demetrius swears his innocence, but the distressed Hermia rushes away to find the man with whom she is really in love. Realizing that the pursuit is hopeless, Demetrius lies down and falls asleep. Oberon squeezes the love juice on his eyes.

'Lord, what fools these mortals be!' Puck's comment reminds us of his sheer delight in mischief. Great confusion has already been caused between the four lovers, and more will follow. Puck revels in their 'fond pageant', and now he sees Lysander, suffering from the extreme illusion of his love for Helena, enter in pursuit of her. Lysander is entirely serious, full of passion and protestation. Helena, for her part, is confused and angry. We should remember the compromising position she is in. She is a young and aristocratic lady who has pursued the man she loves into the forest outside Athens. There are great dangers here both to her well-being and to her reputation. Things have also gone disastrously wrong for her. All she wanted was to have a glimpse of the man she loves, and now she is being hotly pursued by another. We must appreciate the seriousness and pain that this causes, at the same time as we laugh at the sheer absurdity of her plight.

Almost at once the absurdity becomes more confused. The noisy confrontation between Lysander and Helena wakes Demetrius. The juice that Oberon poured on his eyes takes effect. He sees Helena, the woman whom he had once wooed successfully and then jilted. Immediately he declares his passionate love for her. His phrases are, if anything, more excessive than those of Lysander. Demetrius now sees the woman he has so recently scorned as a goddess, a perfect and divine woman, beautiful and wholly inspiring. Once again the passion expressed here is both extreme and ridiculous. But we should consider Helena's position. Poor girl, not only is she being chased by Lysander, a state of affairs which baffles her completely. She is now also target of the affections of the man who once abandoned her. If the set-up is comic, it is also touched with a certain cruelty. This is made clear by Helena's speech. She is utterly bewildered by what has happened, and can only assume that the young men have ganged up together to tease her. She believes that they have 'set against me for your merriment'. A cruel trick has been played on her, and it seems to have been orchestrated by the young men themselves. Of course she is wholly unaware that the real cause is the mischievous interference of Oberon and Puck. She rounds on her tormentors. They cannot be gentlemen if they behave in this way. She knows – or thinks she knows – that both young men really hate her from the bottom of their hearts. After all, they are rivals for the love of Hermia. She chides them for the ignoble cruelty of their behaviour. All they have succeeded in doing, she believes, is reducing a harmless and already unhappy girl to tears.

But Helena is not the only one to be confused. Lysander, who is himself acting under the influence of the juice that Oberon has squeezed on his eyes, turns to Demetrius. He does not realize that Demetrius has received similar treatment at the hands of Oberon, and so he does not understand that Demetrius's fervour for the woman he once reviled is the result of an illusion. It seems to Lysander that, as Helena says, Demetrius is being truly unkind. After all, we know perfectly well that he loves – or loved – Hermia. He told everybody so in the first scene. Lysander then adds that since he himself is no longer in love with Hermia – the woman with whom such a short time ago he had resolved to flee – Demetrius can have the girl. Lysander yields to him all claims to Hermia's love. Demetrius, for his part, should yield all his rights in Helena to the newly love-smitten Lysander.

Helena's one-line speech (l. 168) reveals her disgust at what is going on. It is important to imagine the effect of this scene in the theatre. Two passionate young men, acting under an illusion, appear to be making complete fools of themselves while cruelly taunting Helena. She suffers but, although we sympathize with her, we are also moved to laughter. The two young men again try to resolve the position they find themselves in, and at this moment Hermia enters. She has been abandoned by Lysander – his new illusory love for Helena has caused him to leave the woman he once loved alone in the dangerous and threatening wood. We should see the strong element of callousness in the fickle behaviour of these young men.

Hermia has been looking for Lysander and has now found him. It is too dark for her to see him clearly but, as she tells us, she has detected his presence by the sound of his voice. She upbraids Lysander for abandoning her. He turns to her and asks why he should stay with her when his love presses him to go. Again, the callous note is sounded. If Helena was confused by what has happened, so now is Hermia. Lysander, the young man who loved her and vowed to run away with her, now suddenly appears to love her no longer. She cannot understand what has happened: 'What love could press Lysander from my side?' We in the audience know the reason. It is that the juice which Oberon has squeezed on Lysander's eyes has caused him to fall in love with Helena. We are amused because we know what has happened – the characters, however, never understand that they are the victims of Puck and Oberon. They think that their emotions are true and valid ones. We know that they are illusions created by the fairies.

Lysander now speaks again of his love for Helena. He declares, in accordance with convention, that the woman he adores is more beautiful than all the stars in the night sky. Hermia simply cannot believe what she is hearing.

Helena too is bewildered. The only reasonable interpretation of what has happened which she can think of is that not only have Lysander and Demetrius ganged up against her, but Hermia also is 'one of this confederacy'. She believes that all three of them have joined together to taunt her. Her suffering is considerable at this point. She believes herself the victim of arbitrary cruelty. Naturally, she turns on her friend. How could Hermia possibly have joined in with these fickle and callous young men, when the two girls have been the closest friends since their early childhood? The distraught Helena gives a delightful picture of how, as schoolgirls, they used to work together on the same piece of embroidery. To Helena they were like twins: 'two lovely berries moulded on one stem.' Did all this trust and love mean nothing? It seems to Helena that Hermia is determined to 'rent our ancient love asunder' with her disgraceful behaviour. Indeed, Hermia is no better than the two young men who have deliberately set out to tease her.

For her part, Hermia cannot understand a word that Helena is saying. She has not acted in the way that Helena describes at all. She is not part of a plot hatched by Lysander and Demetrius. She knows of no such plot. Indeed, she is probably beginning to think that she is herself a victim of the two young men. After all, the man with whom she has run away, for whom she has abandoned her home and risked her father's lasting displeasure, has just jilted her. It seems highly likely to Hermia that Helena is deliberately scorning *her*. Helena protests. She is the jilted and unhappy woman. Hermia is her rival, the successful woman pursued by both Lysander and her own Demetrius. It seems to Helena that Hermia has deliberately enticed Lysander to tease her, while Hermia has made her 'other love' – and notice how subtly Shakespeare suggests Helena's jealousy – to scorn her with cruel and tasteless vows of love. The only reasonable conclusion, as far as Helena is concerned, is that Hermia is behind the whole plot. Despite Hermia's protestation, Helena thinks she is being deliberately mocked. Her feelings are bitter and intense. Perhaps, as she seems to confess (l. 243), the fault is partly hers – after all, it was she who made sure that Demetrius should follow Lysander and Hermia into the wood. In her desperate state she sees 'death or absence' as the only ways out: she must either commit suicide or run away. She turns to go, but the passionate Lysander begs her to stay. Her disbelieving fury breaks out as she rounds on him: 'O, excellent!' Hermia begs Lysander – the man whom she loves and who she thinks loves her back – not to scorn Helena in this way. Demetrius, now Lysander's rival for Helena's hand, declares that he will fight Lysander. Lysander mocks him, and the two begin to quarrel. The scene is complex, delightful and utterly ridiculous. When Hermia tries to interpose, she only receives more insults.

Again, we may pause to ask ourselves what sort of behaviour it is that we are seeing from these two young men. They are convinced of their own excellence and ardour. We may well be amused but we must also see how strong but illusory passion forces them to treat their lovers in a deplorable way. They hurl crude abuse at the women they once believed to be goddesses, and they are determined to fight with each other.

Just as Helena has been teased to the point of tears, so Hermia is hurt and utterly bewildered. She turns to Lysander (l. 271) and showers him with questions. What is going on? What has changed the Lysander who once loved her? She is still beautiful. Can he really be serious? Lysander says that he is. To the woman whom he has inveigled away from her father's house, in the middle of the forest and the dark of the night, he calmly announces: 'I do hate thee and love Helena.' Hermia is furious and turns back on Helena. As far as she can understand matters, Helena has 'stolen' Lysander's love. Helena is furious at this suggestion. 'Fie, fie, you counterfeit, you puppet, you!'

A wonderfully comic argument now breaks out between the two women. The jealous and jilted Hermia thinks she understands what is going on. Helena has called her a puppet because Hermia is shorter than her. Evidently this makes Helena the more attractive of the two. In her wounded pride, Hermia lets forth a torrent of abuse. She may indeed be the shorter of the two, Helena may be a 'painted maypole', but Hermia is quite prepared to scratch her eyes out. On the stage, Hermia's sudden and very realistic viciousness is hilarious. Helena, distraught, looks to the young men for protection – after all, they both claim to be passionately in love with her. Besides, she is terrified of Hermia's temper. Just because she is taller than Hermia, it does not mean that she can fight with somebody 'something lower' than she is. Hermia explodes with fury at this: 'Lower? Hark, again!' Helena tries to question her livid friend. She insists that she is not part of a conspiracy against Hermia. She has always been faithful to her, kept her secrets, never wronged her. The only thing she has ever done is to send Demetrius off into the wood in pursuit of her and Lysander. Honestly and rather sadly, Helena tells Hermia she followed Demetrius 'for love'. We have known from the start of the play that she is ready to follow Demetrius like a loyal spaniel. Her plan has gone horribly wrong:

> But he hath chid me hence, and threatened me
> To strike me, spurn me – nay, to kill me too.

> (ll. 312–13)

All she wants to do now is to go home. She begs Hermia to let her return to Athens and 'bear my folly back'. She will not interfere any more. She recognizes that she has been foolish and simply wants to go away.

Hermia tells her to get going in no uncertain terms. What is stopping Helena from running back home? Helena replies that only her 'foolish heart' is keeping her. And who has her heart, asks Hermia imperiously – is it with Lysander? 'With Demetrius,' replies Helena. She remains pathetically faithful to him. Lysander and Demetrius both now declare that they will protect Helena. This is particularly ironic in view of the careless contempt with which Demetrius treated Helena earlier on in the play (I I, i). But Helena realizes that she needs all the protection she can get. She is clearly afraid of Hermia, who, though she may be shorter, is a 'vixen'. Hermia is once more roused to fury by this reference to her height. She turns to Lysander – the man she loves and who she thought loved her – and begs him not to let her be insulted in this way. Lysander's reply is an excellent example of the callous contempt with which we see both young men treat their women once they have jilted them:

> Get you gone, you dwarf,
> You minimus of hindering knot-grass made,
> You bead, you acorn.

(ll. 327–9)

Demetrius is made furiously jealous by this, and the two young men chase each other off stage, spoiling for a fight. Hermia and Helena are briefly left alone on stage together. Hermia blames Helena for all her problems. Helena is still afraid. The shorter woman may have quicker hands, but the taller one has longer legs. She uses them to run away. The poor, bewildered Hermia also runs off.

This marvellously farcical argument has been watched by its instigators: Oberon and Puck, who now come forward. Oberon is bewildered and rather angry at what has happened and he rounds on Puck. Puck justifies himself – he squeezed the juice of the flower on to the eyes of a young man dressed in 'Athenian garments'. He did not know that there were two such young men roving round the forest. Besides, he has had much pleasure from the confusion he has caused.

Oberon is more serious. He realizes that the forthcoming fight between Lysander and Demetrius is no joke. After all, Oberon's real role is to be benevolent towards human beings. The last thing that he wants is to start a fight to the death. With fine, evocative poetry, he bids Puck cover the starry night sky with a fog and then mislead both

Lysander and Demetrius. We learned before (II, i, 39) that Puck thoroughly enjoys misleading 'night-wanderers'. Now his master has ordered him to do so. Oberon commands Puck to confuse and exhaust Lysander and Demetrius so much that they will eventually fall asleep. Then Oberon will crush into Lysander's eyes the herb which, as he has told us, will act as a counter-charm to the first one. Lysander will be stripped of his illusions. Oberon's second herb will make Lysander's 'eyeballs roll with wonted sight'. All the harm will be undone, and the very real anguish that the young lovers have been through will seem nothing more than 'a dream and fruitless vision'. All will be made well, and the lovers can go back to Athens and be married. While Puck is dealing with Lysander and Demetrius, Oberon will himself go and beg the little Indian boy from Titania, squeeze the juice of the second herb on her eyes, release her from her illusory love of Bottom, and 'all things shall be peace'.

Puck declares that they should act quickly – dawn is coming, and the ghosts are all trooping home. But as Oberon tells him they themselves are 'spirits of another sort'. These fairies have no associations with evil and death. They are kindly – if mischievous – and their business in the world is to help mankind. Oberon's speech (ll. 388–95) is a superb evocation of the beautiful and kindly forces of nature with which he is at one. None the less, he has a lot to do before the harm that he and Puck have inflicted can be undone, and he leaves to find Titania. Meanwhile Puck will thoroughly enjoy playing a last trick on Lysander and Demetrius. He confuses them by mimicking their voices to each other so that they pursue each other through the wood until they collapse exhausted. On the stage, this is a brilliant opportunity for farce. Lysander and Demetrius are made to look utterly absurd – perhaps they deserve to be laughed at in this way before they are reconciled to the women whom they truly love.

Now Helena enters. She has bravely tried to get back to Athens on her own, but failed. She is lost and bewildered, and decides to lie down on the ground, go to sleep and wait until morning. Three of the bewildered lovers are now on stage and asleep. Puck is waiting for one more to enter – Hermia. She arrives, 'curst and sad'. She too has been wandering alone and frightened round the forest. She is soaked with dew, scratched by briars and so tired that she cannot go another step. As Puck's rhyme says:

> Cupid is a knavish lad
> Thus to make poor females mad.
>
> (ll. 440–41)

All four young people are now asleep on the floor of the forest. Puck steals over to Lysander and squeezes the antidote to Oberon's charm on his eyes. When he wakes, Lysander will fall in love with Hermia once again. It is important to note that this counter-charm is not squeezed on to Demetrius's eyes. He will continue to love Helena.

## ACT IV SCENE i

If the aristocratic lovers are now in a sleep from which they will wake to find their true partners, down-to-earth Bottom is still part of the most beautiful dream the play has to offer. Titania, the Queen of the Fairies, is still passionately in love with the very ordinary Athenian whom the mischievous Puck has half-transformed into an ass. Titania draws her lover to her 'flowery bed'. She brushes his cheeks, decks his head with muskroses and kisses his ears. Of course, we laugh. If this is a comic scene on the stage, it is also beautiful to behold and rather touching. Bottom's four fairy attendants are summoned to him and scratch his head or bring him honey. Titania asks him if he would care to hear the music of Fairyland. Bottom wants to hear 'the tongs and the bones'. All the magic of Titania cannot purge this simple man's common tastes – he prefers crude and lively folksong to what the poet Tennyson called 'the horns of elfland faintly blowing'. Titania asks him if he would like something to eat. Bottom wants to 'munch your good dry oats'. He would like nothing more than this or a handful of hay. He is offered greater treats, but – half-ass that he is – he would prefer 'dried pease'. He is getting tired: 'I have an exposition of sleep come upon me.' As he falls asleep, the Fairy Queen winds him in her arms. It is an image of greatest tenderness and poetry, as well as wonderful absurdity.

It is just this absurdity that Oberon relishes. He has wanted revenge on Titania, and now he has it. He has humiliated her to his satisfaction. Now he begins to pity her. He tells Puck that he has watched Titania wooing Bottom before now and, while she did so, cruelly taunted her. So besotted with her new love was she, that she even agreed to surrender the Indian boy to Oberon in return for being left alone. Oberon now has all he wants: the little Indian boy and revenge on his wife. It is time for him to remove 'this hateful imperfection of her eyes'. He also tells Puck to remove the ass's head, so that Bottom can return to Athens and, like the others:

> ... think no more of this night's accidents
> But as the fierce vexation of a dream.

(ll. 67–8)

As Oberon squeezes the antidote on to Titania's eyes, she wakes. She thinks she must have been dreaming: she was 'enamoured of an ass'. Oberon points to Bottom, who is still sleeping, and Titania is appalled. The effect of Oberon's antidote is to remove her love from Bottom and return it to him. Music is called for, and the newly reconciled Titania and Oberon dance to its ravishing sound as Puck removes the ass's head from Bottom's neck.

Once more, it is important that we imagine the effect of this scene on the stage. The music should be serene, an expression of harmony and order. The values of harmony and order are also symbolized in the regal and stately dance of Oberon and the Queen. This moment of reconciliation is a splendid prelude to the end of the play: the reconciliation of the four young lovers and the celebration of their marriages, along with that of Theseus and Hippolyta. As the dance ends, dawn breaks. The fairies trip lightly away, as Titania begs an explanation of what has happened.

The music of Fairyland is rudely shattered by the noise of Theseus's hunting horns. Dreaming and illusion are over now. The night has passed, and it is in the light of day that the human lovers will finally untangle their problems and resolve their differences with one another. The hunting horns, the baying of the dogs and the arrival of the commanding figure of Theseus returns us to the human world. Light and human activity replace the mischief and magic of the fairy world.

The discussion of hunting and its excitement form a strong contrast to what we have just seen. Despite all the noise, the four young lovers have been so exhausted by the night's complications that even the hunting horns fail to wake them. Theseus glimpses them asleep on the ground and Egeus totters forward and recognizes them in complete amazement: 'I wonder of their being here together.' Theseus evidently has his own ideas about why four young people should be found asleep in the wood. As he quickly and rather tactfully remarks to Egeus:

> No doubt they rose up early to observe
> The rite of May ...

> (ll. 131–2)

He goes on to remind Egeus that Hermia must today make up her mind whether she is going to marry the man of her father's choice, live as a nun, or submit to the death penalty. Theseus summons in his huntsmen to wake the sleeping lovers with the sound of their hunting horns. Lysander is the first to wake. He is the lover on whose eyes Oberon has squeezed the antidote to his first charm, and he will fall back in love with Hermia. Half asleep though he is, he recognizes that he has been found by the ruler of Athens in an extremely compromising position. He begs Theseus's pardon. Puzzled, and no doubt slightly amused, Theseus asks Lysander what has been happening. Lysander – still half asleep – says he is far from certain. Then, as he begins to wake, he remembers the plot that he hatched with Hermia, and confesses to Theseus that he was stealing away from Athens to elope with Hermia. Egeus breaks in furiously. Lysander has condemned himself out of his own mouth. Egeus demands revenge 'upon his head' – he has been ignored, and wants legal retribution from Theseus. Demetrius – the young man Egeus wants his daughter Hermia to marry – now speaks up. He confesses that Helena told him of Lysander's and Hermia's plot, that he followed them into the wood, and that Helena followed him. None the less, he is at a loss to explain what has happened to his feelings. He pursued Hermia because he thought he was truly in love with her. Now – and he cannot explain how it has come to pass – he is in love with Helena. His affections have returned to the woman he jilted. He can only account for this by saying that his tastes have matured. We must smile at the honourable change of heart, back to the woman to whom he proposed: we know that Demetrius is still undergoing the effects of the love potion that Oberon squeezed on his eyes.

In some respects Demetrius is still suffering from an illusion. But it is a benevolent illusion. The fickle young man who has behaved so callously now has the opportunity of righting the wrong that he has done. He has returned to the love of the woman whom he betrayed, and we should be so happy to see justice done that we will keep the secret.

Love has triumphed. Lysander has returned to loving the woman for whom he was prepared to risk everything. Demetrius is in love with the girl he was so cruel to before. Theseus recognizes that such claims as these have more force than Egeus's wishes. It is simply natural justice that Demetrius should be excused from his promise to marry Hermia, and allowed instead to marry the woman whom he once loved and whom he now loves again. Furthermore, Lysander's love for Hermia is clearly so strong that to deny it would be very cruel indeed. Theseus – whose authority as Duke of Athens we have come to respect – overrules Egeus's wishes and declares that all four will be married to those they have chosen. There are three happy weddings to look forward to. Having settled matters for the lovers, Theseus, Hippolyta, Egeus and the hunting party leave them on the stage together.

As the lovers turn to each other, the events of the night before seem to them like a dream. Indeed, Demetrius wonders whether they are awake or whether they are still sleeping. So does Helena, who feels that Demetrius is now 'mine own and not mine own'. To the audience, this is an interesting comment, for we know that Helena has now had her lover restored to her, but we also know – as she does not – that it is wholly the result of Oberon's benevolent magic. Helena's remark is truer than she realizes. When the lovers come slowly to their senses, they remember that Egeus, Theseus and Hippolyta have been with them in the wood, and that Theseus has ordered them to follow him to the temple where he is to celebrate his marriage. All four lovers now leave, and Demetrius suggests that they should recount their dreams to each other on the way. We are left wondering how much sense they will make of them.

Only Bottom is left on the stage. He too is beginning to wake up. As he comes to his senses, he thinks of the play that he and his companions hope to perform in front of the Duke. For the moment, his concern about the play is more vivid to him than his memory of his encounter with Titania. Then, gradually, the memories of the fantastic liaison return to him. His soliloquy, as he tries to piece together the experiences he can remember, is both touching and very funny. In his own words, Bottom has had 'a most rare vision'. Indeed, it has been the most poetic vision of the whole play. This ordinary man has spent the night beside the Fairy Queen. So marvellous are the dim memories of this to Bottom that he can scarcely believe them. The contents of the 'dream' are beyond his powers to explain. We should bear in mind the effect of his speech in the theatre. As Bottom pieces his fragments of memory together, we should perhaps imagine him lifting his hands to where his ass's ears were and finding that they have disappeared. Perhaps he reaches out to touch his ass's nose as well. As he tries to recount his dream, once again his language becomes marvellously confused. He talks of the eye hearing, the ear seeing, the hand tasting and the tongue thinking. This is both broadly comic and an effective way of suggesting how bewildering to him Bottom's memories are. He is determined Peter Quince should write a ballad (or popular poem) about the vision, which should 'be called "Bottom's Dream", because it hath no bottom'. With touching loyalty he considers that Quince's ballad will enhance the mechanicals' play. Promising to sing the ballad himself before the Duke, Bottom leaves the stage.


## ACT IV SCENE ii

The other mechanicals meanwhile are very worried. The choice of play to perform before Theseus must be made soon. But no one can find Bottom. As Flute says: 'If he come not, then the play is marred.' All the mechanicals are convinced that Bottom – the great ham actor – is the only man in Athens capable of performing in the role of Pyramus. Snug enters to tell his fellows that the Duke and 'two or three lords and ladies' have now been married. This makes things seem worse to the mechanicals. If only they had found Bottom, their play would have been chosen and they would have 'all been made men'. In Flute's opinion, Bottom would have merited a pension of at least sixpence a day for performing the role of Pyramus, the tragic lover.

Bottom appears, and the others are thrilled to see him. He begins to tell them that he has something marvellous to recount. He is 'to discourse wonders' to them. Obviously, we think that he is going to tell the other mechanicals about his dream. However, what Bottom in fact has to say is something quite different. He bids all the mechanicals get their costumes together, learn their lines and meet up at Theseus's palace: 'For the short and the long is, our play is preferred.' A theatrical triumph seems to be in the offing. Bottom, ever keen to ensure the highest theatrical standards, asks the actors to refrain from eating onions and garlic so that their breath will be sweet. With their good news, the mechanicals hurry excitedly away.

## ACT V SCENE i

We return to Theseus and the noble lovers. The four young people have been telling Theseus and Hippolyta about their adventures in the wood. Hippolyta finds what they have to say very strange; Theseus counters that their story is 'more strange than true'. He thinks that the heat of their love has excited their imaginations. Love has driven them to the edge of sanity and made them poets, people who live in a world of the imagination. Theseus elaborates this idea in a beautiful and well-known speech where he says:

> The lunatic, the lover, and the poet
> Are of imagination all compact.

> (ll. 7–8)

Theseus understands that the imagination is a hectic and inventive force, creating fantasies and illusions, errors and delights. What he says is quite true, but we in the audience know far more of what has happened to the lovers than they do or Theseus does. We have been shown the magical world of Fairyland and its mischievous but entrancing delights. The lovers have also visited it, but they have no clear recollection of how it operates. Awakened from their dream, they only have guesses and half-memories of the pain and confusion that such a supernatural world provides. Perhaps Hippolyta sees further than Theseus. While she agrees with what he says about the powers of the imagination, she realizes that the young lovers' story suggests something more than mere imagination – it 'more witnesseth than fancy's images'. There seems to her to be some truth underlying it – a truth which, however, she is not able fully to understand.

At this moment the young newlyweds enter. No longer do they belong to the world of Puck and Oberon, of magic and the imagination. They have returned to Athens and happy, ordinary human life. Theseus asks them what entertainment they would all like 'between our after-supper and bedtime.' He summons Philostrate and asks him what diversions have been arranged. Philostrate provides him with a list, which Theseus reads out, dismissing each of the performances until he comes to that of Bottom and the mechanicals. The first entertainment mentioned is *The Battle with the Centaurs*, which is a story Theseus has already recounted to Hippolyta. The next 'device' he has seen before, while the third entertainment appears to be a satire, and Theseus does not believe that this is suitable for 'a nuptial ceremony'. There remains only the dramatic offering of Bottom and his friends. This is described as:

> A tedious brief scene of young Pyramus
> And his love Thisbe; *'very tragical mirth'*.
>
> (11. 56–7)

The courtiers evidently find the mechanicals' confused description of their own play extremely funny. Indeed, they will laugh throughout at the inadequacy of its language (see p. 80). Theseus is also amused by the idea of 'very tragical mirth', and he turns to Philostrate for an explanation. The sophisticated Philostrate is contemptuous: he tells Theseus that the play is indeed 'brief', but is none the less so bad that it is surely 'tedious'. Both the language and the actors are inadequate to the subject they are to portray. In their play, the death of Pyramus is far from tragic: indeed, when he saw a rehearsal, Philostrate laughed until he wept. In response to Theseus's question, Philostrate describes the actors as 'hard-handed men that work in Athens here'. They have no experience of acting whatsoever. They are merely ordinary people and certainly quite unsuited to performing a wedding masque before the ruler of Athens. The noble Theseus none the less declares that he will hear the play. He dismisses Philostrate's objections to it and, showing the humane nature which has characterized him throughout the play, states there can be nothing wrong with the mechanicals' performance if it is an expression of their honest simplicity and loyalty to him. Philostrate goes to summon the actors.

Hippolyta is troubled by the thought of seeing worthy men making fools of themselves. Theseus overrides these objections too, by telling her that he has seen the most learned men 'shiver and look pale' when they have planned to deliver him long and pompous speeches of welcome. In Theseus's experience of such events he has to pick a welcome out of the embarrassed silence into which such men often fall. He is more concerned to appreciate the love and duty that underlie such performances than the quality of the performances themselves. Now that he has demonstrated his humanity, Theseus settles down with his court to watch the mechanicals' performance.

The play-within-the-play begins grandly enough with a flourish of trumpets. Quince steps forward. What happens now is ludicrous: Quince rattles through the speech with which he hopes to introduce the performance, getting all his full-stops or 'points' confused, so the sense comes out exactly the opposite of what he intends. Once again we laugh at the confused way in which the mechanicals handle the language which they hope is grand. At the end of Quince's speech, Theseus and Hippolyta joke about its quality. And throughout the rest of the performance all the newlyweds will make rather thinly comic and unkind comments about the performance they are watching. It is important to be attuned to this. The play which Bottom and his fellows perform is indeed hilariously funny. It is funny because it deals with a grand and tragic subject in a hopelessly inadequate way. None the less, we have come to be very fond of Bottom and his fellows, and although we may laugh at them as they stumble through their performance, our laughter cannot be harsh. We are both amused and moved as, indeed, we have been throughout the play. Our laughter should be a warm and kindly laughter. In this respect our reaction is completely different from the amusement of the court, which seems, by contrast, to suggest something of the artificiality and even the callousness that the young lovers showed in the wood. As they ridicule the efforts of Bottom and his friends, we come to appreciate the comedy and pathos of the mechanicals' performance more and more.

Quince next tells the audience who the actors represent, and the whole plot of the play they are to perform. Clearly there will be no dramatic tension here, no excitement or surprise. We are also reminded once again that the language of the performance will be truly ridiculous. Quince's speech is obviously designed to impress the noble audience with the power of poetry. In fact, it only makes us laugh. It tries to be sublime but succeeds in being absurd – this is known as 'bathos'. A particularly good example of how the language of the prologue fails comes when Quince tries to impress us with alliteration, or repeated consonants:

> *Whereat with blade – with bloody, blameful blade –*
> *He bravely broached his boiling bloody breast.*
>
> (ll. 145–6)

The courtiers joke as Quince departs with the other actors, and then Snug shuffles on dressed up as the Wall. A walking wall is ridiculous enough; a talking one is quite absurd. None the less, it is vital that we imagine the play in performance here – real comic actors can make this scene truly hilarious. But the best is yet to come.

Bottom now enters to glory in his tragic role. If the language of Quince's prologue was absurd, then Bottom's speech is even more so. Bottom grandly invokes the night and curses the wall that separates him from his beloved Thisbe. At this moment it becomes evident that Snout has forgotten to hold up his two fingers to suggest the cranny in the wall through which the two lovers are supposed to speak. He now does so and Bottom thanks him. The great tragic actor looks through the gap that has been so conveniently provided for him and curses the wall because he cannot see his Thisbe. Theseus wittily comments that since the wall can talk, it should curse Bottom back. This is too much for Bottom. He turns to the audience and, breaking the dramatic illusion (see pp. 81–6), tells them that what he has just said is the cue for Thisbe to enter. The audience is not to worry, the play will proceed exactly as it is supposed to. Young Flute now comes on stage – in a good production his mere appearance should be enough to make us laugh; we can picture him in a ridiculous female costume. The absurdity of his lines will certainly amuse us. The lovers enjoy a silly dialogue in which they promise to meet at what they still wrongly call 'Ninny's tomb'. They leave, and Snout, in a fine comic moment, looks across at the audience and says that now he has played his part as Wall it is time for him to go as well. The wall walks off the stage. As Hippolyta says: 'This is the silliest stuff that ever I heard.' Theseus kindly excuses the inadequacies of the play, insisting once again that the courtly audience appreciate the good intention of the actors.

Snug and Starveling enter, dressed as Lion and Moonshine respectively. In case the ladies in the audience should be frightened of Snug dressed as the Lion, he proceeds to tell them that he is not really a lion at all, just Snug the joiner, dressed up. Once again the dramatic illusion is completely wrecked. The Duke and the court are amused by this speech, but become even more critical of the appearance of Starveling as Moonshine. Starveling begins his speech by trying to explain his costume, using the pompous language characteristic of the play-within-the-play. However, the newlyweds are so amused by his appearance, and joke so loudly about it, that Starveling is obliged to stand still and be silent. Evidently he is very put out by this, and we see extremely bad manners on the part of the Duke and his court. When Lysander asks him to continue, he looks them straight in the face and tells them in his own person what he represents. Starveling thinks that he cannot make himself understood in the language of the play, and so steps out of character to speak as Starveling the tailor. Flute, still dressed as Thisbe, now enters to keep her promised appointment at 'Ninny's tomb'. The Lion roars and Thisbe runs off in terror. The Lion tears her mantle as she runs away and a fragment of it remains on the ground for Pyramus to discover. A small trace of Thisbe's blood stains the cloth.

Bottom comes on as Pyramus. His speech is an example of pure bathos. Once again his language becomes hopelessly confused, while, when he discovers the fragment of blood-stained material, his poetry is as flat as it possibly could be. Instead of the heroic ranting of a tragic lover, we hear words which are laughable. Pyramus, of course, thinks that his lover has been killed by a lion. In his despair he vows to commit suicide. He draws his sword and runs the blade through himself. No doubt we should picture him very obviously running the blade between his arm and his chest. Now – dead – he proceeds to talk to the audience. Nothing could be more absurd, unless it be the gross over-acting that Bottom indulges in as he staggers across the stage pretending to die.

The play requires that Thisbe arrive to discover the body of Pyramus. Flute enters on cue. He sees the dead body of Pyramus and walks over to it. The heroine's speech of tragic despair is once again ludicrous. At the end of the play, Theseus remarks, 'Moonshine and Lion are left to bury the dead.' Demetrius reminds him that Wall is still alive, but at this moment Pyramus, who is supposed to be dead, starts up and tells them that the wall has been destroyed. He then asks if his noble audience would like to 'see the epilogue' or be provided with a dance. Theseus replies that the play needs no epilogue, since the actors are all dead and there is no one to blame. Theseus is trying to suppress his laughter at the absurd play that he has watched, but he none the less manages to convince his loyal subjects that they have performed excellently. The play was, he declares, 'very notably discharged'. However, the idea of these actors reciting an epilogue is more than he can bear, and he bids them dance instead. We should probably imagine what follows as an energetic, amusing and honest piece of folk-dancing. It should be something which makes us forget the absurdity of the mechanicals' play, and which at the same time suggests their loyalty and natural high spirits. We might also like to compare its rough country vigour to the delights of the dance which Oberon and Titania performed when they were reconciled with each other. That dance suggested peace and loving harmony. The dance of Bottom and his fellows does the same, but in a comic way.

When the dance is over a bell sounds. It is midnight, time for the lovers to go to bed. Theseus announces that the celebration of their marriages will last for a full fortnight. With this promise, all the newlyweds – Theseus and Hippolyta, Demetrius and Helena, Lysander and Hermia – leave the stage. The moment should suggest human happiness and fulfilment.

The stage is not left bare. Although we have seen the human lovers for the last time, Puck now enters to remind us of the fairy world, the world of nature and of kindly magic. Puck's speech (ll. 361–80) evokes the feeling of the supernatural and the benevolent, the care and consideration of the fairies for human welfare. In what should perhaps be the most beautiful visual spectacle in a play full of such images, Oberon and Titania appear with their fairy servants. The darkness of midnight has enveloped Theseus's palace. It is to this realm of the humans that the fairies have now come. No longer are they the powerful and mischievous spirits of the wood outside Athens. They are benevolent beings, come to provide their little services to the human world. We should imagine them bearing lights or candles. Oberon orders them to carry their lights through the house. He tells them that they should sing as they go about their business, and Titania bids them rehearse their song first. A final dance takes place on the stage before us. It should be a scene of great beauty, great imaginative power. It should suggest all the benevolence and magic which the fairies are bringing to the home of the humans. Once more it is a dance of love, of reconciliation and of kindly feelings. The dance shows us – as does the speech of Oberon which follows – that in the realm of the humans the fairies are servants. They are not here to delight in trickery; they have come to Theseus's house – as Oberon reminds them – to bless it. He has the power to bless all three marriages, to make sure that they are loving and secure and that the children which come from them will be perfect in every way. Now the fairies 'trip away'. They have become little, loyal creatures devoted to man's well-being.

At the end of the performance, Puck steps forward to address the audience. We have seen that *A Midsummer Night's Dream* is a play much concerned with illusion (see also pp. 81–6). We have seen the illusions under which the lovers are obliged to suffer during their stay in the wood. They themselves think that the experiences partake of the nature of a dream. We have also seen Bottom and his friends trying to present a play, a dramatic illusion. Finally, we in the audience are made aware that we have been part of an illusion, a dream. Shakespeare and the actors have conjured up an illusory, beautiful and comic world for us; but, like everything else in the play, it has no real substance. It too is an illusion. It is just this illusion which Puck breaks. As he steps forward, he begins to step out of his role. He asks us to imagine that, if we have not enjoyed the play, it is nothing more than a dream. If we have enjoyed it, however, the actor playing Puck asks us to applaud him and the other actors who have created the illusion in front of our eyes. Just as the lovers in the wood woke from their illusory dreams to the sound of Theseus's hunting horns, so we too will dispel the magical illusion of *A Midsummer Night's Dream* by loudly applauding the actors who created it.

# *Characters*

## THESEUS

Theseus opens the play and he is presented throughout as a man of wise and kindly authority. At the start he is about to be married to Hippolyta, the Queen of the Amazons. He has won his bride in a battle against the Amazonian forces but although he courted Hippolyta 'with my sword', he will wed her 'with pomp, with triumph, and with revelling'. His first speeches help to suggest that marriage will be seen in the play as the mature and proper end of love.

Theseus is the ruler of Athens, and hence responsible for maintaining its laws, one of which appears to be cruel. When old Egeus demands that his daughter face up to the punishment that will be inflicted on her if she does not marry Demetrius, Theseus not only explains that custom requires that she will either die or live as a nun if she does not obey her father, but he also prompts her in a kindly way to think carefully about the decision she must make. He impresses on her how difficult a life of chaste seclusion would be for a young girl. He also checks Egeus's haste, and gives Hermia four more days in which to make up her mind. Theseus's kindly interest in his subjects is also made clear when he bids Demetrius and Egeus go along with him for 'some private schooling' (I, i, 116). Theseus clearly regards it as part of his duty to supervise the happiness and welfare of his people.

We come to appreciate the wisdom and generosity of Theseus's character in the later parts of the play. When the four lovers have been through their painful experiences in the wood and Demetrius has recognized that his true love is for Helena, while Lysander is still in love with Hermia – Theseus decrees that the young people's love for each other must be the basis of their marriages. He overrules Egeus, sets aside the law of Athens, and declares that Hermia shall marry Lysander after all. Theseus's kindly concern for his subjects is shown again when he chooses the mechanicals' play for part of his wedding celebration. Although he is warned by Philostrate that the performance will be a lamentable business, Theseus says that since the performers are true and loyal Athenians who will do their honest best to amuse him, he will watch the piece. He will accept the mechanicals' play in the spirit in which it is offered. Although Theseus is certainly amused by Bottom and his crew, his consideration for them is touching.

It is possible, then, to see Theseus as a wise, kindly and mature ruler of his dukedom, as a man of insight and imagination, as a lover and, finally, as a married man. However, it is also important that we realize he is involved in the world of fairies too. We learn from Oberon that Titania particularly favours him and, at the end of the play, when all the marriages have been concluded and the festivities are at an end, Oberon and Titania with their attendant fairies come to bless Theseus's house. Theseus has shown himself throughout the play as a strong and able man, and it is right that at its conclusion his future happiness and prosperity should be guaranteed by the fairy world. As they enter his house, the fairies – who have created so much havoc in the play and appeared as both powerful and mischievous – become little, benevolent spirits wishing joy and prosperity to this fine man.

## HIPPOLYTA

Hippolyta is the Queen of the Amazons. Like Theseus, who has won her in battle, she is a fine and commanding figure capable of love and humane insight. She relishes the prospect of marrying Theseus, and it is she who, at the end of the play, realizes that the experience which the young lovers have undergone, while a strange and admirable thing, may well be connected to the supernatural world.

It is worth noticing that, while she is amused by the mechanicals' play, her comments perhaps show more kindness and imaginative insight than those of the young lovers.

Just as Theseus is connected to the fairy world through Titania, so

Hippolyta has the special regard of Oberon. Like that of her husband, her future happiness is assured by the fairies.

## EGEUS

Egeus is the oldest of the human characters in the play, and is presented as a fussing, unimaginative and rather narrow-minded man. He has resolved that his daughter Hermia should marry Demetrius and, when she refuses, he brings her before Theseus and demands the full penalty of the law. Clearly, Egeus has little sympathy with human love, and when the royal party find all four of the young people asleep on the forest floor, he demands that Athenian law be brought in to punish Lysander. Theseus, a man of far greater imaginative insight, overrules Egeus and so assures that Hermia is finally married to the man that she loves. The contrast between Egeus and Theseus has the effect of helping us to see the humane insight of the ruler of Athens.

## THE LOVERS: HERMIA, LYSANDER, DEMETRIUS, HELENA

It is right to consider the young lovers in the play both as a quartet and as individual people. While on the one hand each of them has unique characteristics, on the other hand they also have much in common. Indeed, many of the confusions arise because they are all – particularly Lysander and Demetrius – so alike.

They are all obviously young, and share experiences of love which are extreme, sometimes cruel and – to us in the audience – continuously amusing. All four of them can use language of the highest and most refined style. When Lysander and Hermia are left alone on stage at the start, we are provided with a beautiful example of highly sophisticated and artificial love talk (I, i). None the less, Shakespeare often chooses to make us laugh at such fine feelings. For instance, when Demetrius has had the love potion poured on his eyes and falls hopelessly in love with Helena (III, ii), his language is again that of the refined and ardent young nobleman. However, far from being moved, we laugh: nothing could be more absurd than such avowedly sincere statements uttered by a young man suffering from an illusion. Further, while all four young people are capable of refined sentiment, they can be also callous and quarrelsome. Lysander and Demetrius may well think their fine phrases of love suggest nobility and ardour. None the less it is true that when they decide to jilt the women with whom they have been in love, then they can treat them with cruel indifference and rather brutal scorn. We may like to compare the way Lysander talks to Hermia in the opening scene with the way he addresses her under the illusion (III, ii, 327–9). We may find below the smoothly polished surface of this fine young gentleman a callous and perhaps even vindictive boy. Such contrast between the language of high passion and the language of contempt and scorn is also apparent in Helena and Hermia. Helena, for example, is capable of the most elaborate and subtle analysis of love (I, i, 226–51). She can reveal the desperate depths of her affection (II, i, 202–10). None the less, in her confrontation with Hermia, we realize that under her sophisticated surface is a woman who can speak her own mind strongly (III, ii). The contrasted styles of language are even more obvious in Hermia. While she can exchange the most beautiful and poetic notions with Lysander, she is also capable of rounding in the most vigorous way on Helena, her childhood friend. Such characteristics – youth, refined ardour, callousness, bluntness and, above all, a frequent inability to see how ludicrous love can be – are common to the four lovers.

If there are obvious similarities between the young lovers, there are also certain points which make them individuals. Hermia, for example, is a brave and forthright girl. She defies her father and, when she does so, the force of her feelings and commitment to Lysander surprise even her. It is these feelings which give Hermia the strength to agree to Lysander's romantic plan of running away from Athens and living together happily where the Athenian law cannot reach them. If Hermia is a strong and brave character, we still laugh at her. The suffering which she endures in the wood when she is abandoned by Lysander is certainly painful to her, but we cannot help also being amused by the absurd problems which she faces. Of course, we laugh at her openly when she is having an argument with her former schoolfriend Helena. Finally, we are delighted and reassured when Theseus arranges matters so that this brave and sincere girl can marry the man with whom she has been in love all along.

Helena at first strikes us as a potentially more tragic figure than her friend Hermia. We are told about her before we meet her. Lysander informs us that Helena was once courted by Demetrius, that she responded to his advances, but that he jilted her for Hermia. In the early parts of the play Helena is the beautiful but rejected woman, suffering from the pangs of hopeless love. She expresses her wretchedness in a powerful and coherent manner. For example, Helena is perfectly well able to see that love is blind, fickle and irresponsible (I, i, 226–51). She also realizes that her dependence on Demetrius is somewhat mawkish. Helena knows that her hopeless love is a humiliating matter, but she recognizes the power of her desperate emotions, and it is she who causes Demetrius to pursue Hermia and Lysander into the wood. Helena does this simply so that she may, in her turn, follow Demetrius and at least be given the happiness of a glimpse of him. Rather naïvely, she believes that she will be able to return to Athens once all the lovers have gathered in the wood. In fact, she will not be able to escape so easily. She will be forced to suffer the humiliating and insulting attentions of both Lysander and Demetrius. Furthermore, she will be left alone in the wood, unable to find her way out. Indeed, one of the chief characteristics which distinguish Helena from Hermia is the greater degree of suffering that Helena has to undergo before she finds married happiness. We should notice one further point – while Lysander returns to his true love of Hermia *after* the love potion has been wiped from his eyes, Demetrius falls back in love with Helena precisely through the power of the magic flower, and this illusion is never removed. We are delighted that Helena finally finds the love of the man she has so doted upon, but we should also accept that Demetrius's love for her is based on an illusion – the power of the juice that has been squeezed into his eyes. Despite the fact that part of their love remains based on illusion, Demetrius and Helena are finally married, and they join the happy chorus of young people at the end of the play on whom Oberon and Titania shower their blessings.

Lysander is first characterized by Egeus as a deceitful young man. Egeus wishes his daughter Hermia to marry Demetrius. However, so effective has Lysander's courtship been, that it is he who has won Hermia's affection. Lysander is in no doubt that the force of his love – and the fact that he believes himself to be quite as good a man as Demetrius – are sufficient reasons for him to marry Hermia. Something underhand about him is perhaps suggested when he tells Theseus and the assembled company that his rival Demetrius wooed and won the love of Helena, before he transferred his affections to Hermia and obtained her father's approval for their marriage. It is Lysander who hatches the romantic but melodramatic plot by which he and Hermia will run away from Athens and live with his rich aunt, where the law can no longer reach them. Although Lysander at first appears as a full-blooded romantic – winning his lover from a preferred rival, hatching a plan to steal away with her, and talking to her with the most refined language – he is, like the other young lovers, a victim of the absurd positions in which love and its illusions can place people. Besides this, his rejection of Hermia – whom he has inveigled into the wood with promises of marriage – is callous and sudden. He cares nothing for Hermia once he has fallen in love with Helena. He may be suffering from an illusion, but we should notice that he is contemptuous, violent and unstable in his behaviour in the wood. He helps to illustrate the point that love can be intense, fickle and absurd. When the charm is removed from his eyes, however, he returns to the woman he has always loved, and it is a tribute to Theseus's wisdom that he should be allowed to marry Hermia against her father's wishes.

Just as Lysander's actions illustrate the irresponsible and sometimes callous nature of love, so does the behaviour of Demetrius. Indeed, it may be possible to think of Demetrius as being slightly more heartless than Lysander. After all, he is not suffering under an illusion when, before the play starts, he jilts Helena and falls in love with Hermia. He is merely an inconstant young man who is quite indifferent to the suffering that he has caused. When he meets Helena in the wood before the charm has been placed on his eyes, he treats her in a very rough and cruel way. He does not care that she has placed herself in danger and in a compromising position for his sake. It is also important to note that when Demetrius joins the band of newlyweds at the end of the play, the force of the revived love he feels for Helena springs entirely from the love potion on his eyes. He is still suffering from an illusion. However, it is an illusion with happy consequences, and we are delighted that he is finally reunited with the woman who has loved him so loyally and doggedly throughout the play.

## PHILOSTRATE

Philostrate is the Master of Theseus's Revels. This means that he is an important court servant, responsible for the Duke's entertainment. He tries to appear a somewhat sophisticated and cynical person. He can only see the ludicrous side of the play that the mechanicals hope to present; it takes the deeper imaginative insight of Theseus to see that the tragedy of Pyramus and Thisbe is a well-meant, if inept, expression of loyalty.

## THE FAIRIES: OBERON, TITANIA, PUCK

The fairies are characterized by the force of their magic, the power of their language, and a delightful combination of mischievousness and goodness. It is important, when we are considering them, that we should imagine the effect they make on the stage. Their visual appearance should be as entrancing and evocative as the words they speak and the music they sing. The fairies provide the play with its imaginative richness and splendour.

Oberon is the King of the Fairies – just as Theseus is the most powerful figure in the human world, so Oberon is the ruler of his. However, whereas Theseus is a man of responsibility and mature insight, Oberon has a more variable and changing character. He is certainly a figure of power, but he also enjoys something of Puck's delight in trickery, while – at the end of the play, and by a brilliant transformation – this marvellously varied character becomes the benevolent little sprite who comes to give happiness and well-being to the human lovers who have been so tormented by the fairies in the wood.

The very real strife caused by Oberon's argument with Titania over the Indian boy is made clear when the two first confront each other (I I, i). We should note that the longer and more evocative speeches here are given to Titania, and that Oberon, by contrast, appears more simply as a jealous and even rather vindictive husband. Certainly, when he is left alone with Puck, he vows to have his revenge. However, it is most important to appreciate the power and sheer beauty of the poetry Oberon utters. Mischief and beauty are rival parts of his character. For example, as he describes to Puck how the flower whose juice he will squeeze on Titania's eyes came to have the power that it does, his descriptions of the sea and the mermaids' music, of the night and the beauty of nature, make us realize that Oberon is magically at one with these forces. Oberon is indeed a supernatural figure enjoying a world of potency and delight very different to that which ordinary mortals know. We should then contrast this to the pleasure that he is going to derive from using the power to get his revenge on Titania. The two apparently contradictory elements in Oberon's character – the supernaturally beautiful world of Fairyland and the almost boyish trickery of those who populate it – are powerfully brought together in the scene where Oberon describes the bank where it is Titania's habit to sleep (I I, i). Oberon is a force of natural beauty and magic, and yet what he wants is to use his power to humiliate his wife. The same speech introduces us to a third important element in Oberon's character – his sense of concern for the human world. He has seen something of the conflicts that the young lovers are undergoing, and now he wishes to help them. Of course, his intervention will in fact be responsible for much of the suffering and comedy of the scenes that take place in the wood.

One aspect of the presentation of Oberon which will be far more obvious in the theatre than on the printed page is the fact that Oberon makes himself invisible – in other words, the human characters cannot see him. Like Puck, who also observes much of the comic entanglement between the young lovers, Oberon derives a great deal of amusement from what he sees. Certainly he thoroughly enjoys seeing the humiliation that Titania is led into once she has fallen in love with Bottom. But we should also appreciate that Oberon is aware of the sufferings that Puck's tricks can cause, and that he works hard to try and set matters right. It is Oberon who makes Puck realize that problems caused by the love potion are serious matters which it is the responsibility of the fairies to sort out (III, ii). This sense of responsibility towards human beings is made most obvious at the end of the play, when the newly reconciled Oberon and Titania dance in Theseus's palace. Though they have caused much suffering to the young lovers, the fairies – now firmly under the control of Oberon – are finally seen as delicate and benevolent little spirits who come to bring peace and prosperity to the world of the humans. However, we should never forget that the power of their language and the beauty of their appearance provide the play with so much of its pure and supernatural beauty, its abiding magic.

Titania is the most gloriously beautiful and evocatively magical character in the play. Her personal beauty, the power of her language, and the visual effect she creates make us realize what a lovely world the fairies inhabit. When we are first introduced to Titania (II, i) her speeches help to provide a most complex range of sensations. We should already have been delighted by the visual effect of her entrance, and to this should be added the obvious resilience of her character. She is quite able to confront Oberon, and she completely refuses to submit to him. She will not hand over the Indian boy. But her language also summons up in the imaginations of the audience the strong and magical way in which the fairies are identified with the forces of nature. It is Titania who creates the marvellous verbal picture through which we see the forces of nature thrown into confusion by the strife that has broken out between her and her husband (II, i, 81–117). Again, in her next speech in the scene, where she gives her reason for refusing to surrender the little Indian boy, she offers us a most evocative picture of the mysterious East, of love, magic, beauty and nature. That Titania can conjure such a fine picture of a rich and desirable world of the imagination is a crucial element of her character. Her language convinces us that she is indeed part of a profoundly beautiful world. This is made clear again in the following scene, which opens as a pageant. Titania has refused to have anything to do with Oberon and has retreated into her own world of beauty. We see its loveliness as she lies down upon her bank and is entertained by fairies until she is lulled to sleep. The visual impact of this scene – and also the music which the fairies sing – should utterly entrance our imaginations. It is vital that they should do so, for only if this scene is really compelling can we appreciate both the contrast of this world with the horny-handed Bottom when he appears, and the marvellous combination of ethereal beauty and pure comedy with which Shakespeare presents us.

To sense the richness of Titania's dallying with Bottom – its mixture of poetry and broad comedy – we need to let our imaginations dwell on the visual quality of the scene while our intellects are amused by its sheer absurdity. Titania lavishes on her ridiculous new-found beloved all the natural delights of her supernatural world. While the delicacy of the way in which Bottom treats the four little fairy servants with whom he is provided is immensely touching, the scenes are also highly sensuous, broadly comic and deeply innocent. And for Oberon, they achieve what he has set out to obtain – the humiliation of Titania and her surrender of the little Indian boy to him. Only when Titania has been through absurdities and humiliations like those which the mortal lovers suffer, can she once more be reconciled with her husband.

It is important to realize that Puck is a figure out of folklore whose real existence many of Shakespeare's audience would have believed in. He is, above all, a mischievous figure. He has little of the sense of grandeur or responsibility which belong to Oberon and Titania. He relishes his magic purely for the pranks that it enables him to perform. It is he who provides the play with most of its feelings of ludicrousness and irresponsibility. It is right that in this comedy Puck should derive most amusement from the sufferings of the lovers and tell the audience: 'Lord, what fools these mortals be!'

Puck's delight in his own mischievousness is clear as soon as we meet him at the opening of the second act. The enthusiasm with which he describes his ability to upset and discomfort simple people shows his character. But we should also see that, despite this, he is the loyal servant of Oberon. Throughout the play, for all Puck's love of sheer uproarious irresponsibility, he does, as dutifully as he can, obey the commands of his master. That these commands get misinterpreted, that the love potion gets squeezed on the eyes of the wrong young man, is not his fault, though he thoroughly enjoys the confusion which results. Again, he takes enormous pleasure in wrecking the rehearsal of the mechanicals' play and, from pure delight in being irresponsible, placing the ass's head on Bottom. In fact, it is just this irresponsible action which allows his master to have his revenge on Titania, for she falls in love with the Bottom whom Puck has so ludicrously transformed. Puck's pleasure at obeying Oberon's commands, and at the same time causing the confusion in which he delights, is made clear when he reports back to Oberon (I I I, ii).

We have seen that much of the comedy in *A Midsummer Night's Dream* is of a farcical variety. Puck has a large part to play in this. For example, he bewilders Lysander and Demetrius when they have vowed to duel with each other, and leads them such a dance through the forest that they eventually lie down and fall asleep from exhaustion. The scene is very amusing to those of us watching it, but there is something more here than sheer farce. Puck certainly enjoys the trouble he is causing the two young men, but we should realize – as Puck almost certainly does not – that this mischief serves a more important purpose. It is part of Oberon's plan of bringing all four young lovers together so that their true married happiness may be assured. Thus, though throughout the play Puck is shown as a delightfully irresponsible figure, he is usually acting under the control of Oberon. And Oberon, as we have seen, not only wishes to reconcile himself to Titania by possessing the little Indian boy, but to serve the mortals and bring them happiness. Puck is an ambiguous figure, then – on the one hand he is thoroughly irresponsible and delights in this, on the other hand his irresponsibility serves a useful purpose. It allows all the characters to go through the adventures and transformations which will eventually bring them to a harmonious conclusion. The four young lovers will marry happily, and their married happiness will be celebrated by the mechanicals' play. Finally, when the lovers are in bed and Theseus's palace is silent, Puck is among the fairies who come to bring it order and harmony.

# THE MECHANICALS: QUINCE, FLUTE, SNOUT, SNUG, STARVELING

The third group of characters in *A Midsummer Night's Dream* is made up of the simple working men of Athens, who have decided to put on a play to celebrate the wedding of Theseus and Hippolyta. As with the other characters in the play, so with the mechanicals, our response to the way in which Shakespeare presents them is complicated. We laugh at them, of course. We cannot fail to be amused by the fact that these well-meaning but relatively uneducated men wish to present a tragic story in dramatic form. The result of their efforts is bathos – their attempt to create noble feelings misfires ludicrously. But, if we laugh at the mechanicals, we cannot fail but to be touched by them also. Indeed, our response to them is very much like that which Theseus urges on his courtiers in the final act. We may be amused, but we should also be moved by the clumsy sincerity of these people.

When we first meet them (I, ii), we learn that Quince is the director of the play and that he has a difficult task keeping his cast in order. Quince, though he is as ignorant as the others, shows himself to be a practical man – he is the one who thinks about the problems of staging the play (I I I, i), although his decisions are ridiculous. We will consider the character of Bottom separately. We should look briefly here at the other characters. Flute, the bellows-mender, has been given the part of Thisbe, a woman's role appropriate to him since his voice has probably not yet broken. Flute is very distressed at having to play a female role, and if we are only reading the play then we need to use all our visual imagination if we are really to appreciate the comedy of his performance in the fifth act. Snug, the joiner, as he admits, is a rather slow-witted man, and he is told that he does not have to learn his lines since he may do his roaring 'extempore'. Snout the tinker is given the ludicrous role of 'Wall' in the play, and much of the comedy here is seeing this man dressed in his costume and shuffling about the stage as a walking, talking wall. Starveling is required to play the role of Moonshine. His most comical moment comes when the courtiers are so amused by his appearance that Starveling seems to lose patience with them and, breaking the dramatic illusion, speaks to them directly in his own words.

## BOTTOM

By far the most fully characterized of the mechanicals is Bottom the weaver. The word 'Bottom', as you will know from your notes, refers to a term in weaving, and only carries a secondary suggestion of 'backside'. Bottom has a most important role in the play. He is one of the few mortal characters who join together the world of the mechanicals, to which he belongs, of the aristocrats, for whom he performs, and of the fairies, by whom he is most wonderfully beguiled.

Bottom above all believes himself to be a great actor. Certainly there is no doubt about his enthusiasm for amateur theatricals. He wishes to take every role in the play (I, ii) and tries to convince Quince of the variety and range of his dramatic talents. But if Bottom enjoys the idea of acting, he does not appreciate that a play is a deliberate illusion. For example, he thinks that the roaring of the lion and the drawing of his sword when he is playing the part of Pyramus will frighten the ladies in the audience. This simple, well-meaning man cannot understand that such ladies are perfectly able to understand that a dramatic performance is an illusion, that it is not literally true. This, of course, is where much of the delight of a play lies. Bottom, however, thinks it necessary actually to explain to his audience that the play they are watching is an illusion. In so doing, he threatens to wreck the drama. We know the events in a play are not true. What is so delightful about the theatre is that we believe the illusions are true while we are watching the play.

Bottom is also involved, however, in the illusory world of the fairies. Puck places an ass's head on him and Titania, under the influence of Oberon's magic flower, awakes to fall passionately in love with him. It is one of the most beautiful and human aspects of the play that this delightful ordinary Athenian is taken to the very heart of the fairy world. He is indeed provided with a 'most rare vision'. It is he who spends the night beside the Fairy Queen. It is Bottom, the man who speaks prose and whose poetry in the play-within-the-play is so absurd, who is none the less given perhaps the most deeply poetic experience in *A Midsummer Night's Dream*. The most beautiful and magical woman imaginable winds her arms around him and offers him the fruits of Fairyland. It is for Bottom to lie beside her in a world of enchanting delight and to be served by Peaseblossom, Cobweb, Moth and Mustard-seed.

The scenes which present Bottom and the Fairy Queen (I I I, i and I V, i) are complicated to describe because they involve so many contradictory emotions. There is, first of all, a strongly sensuous element in them. Titania is presented as a beautiful woman, passionately in love. But we are also obliged to laugh. Titania is suffering under an illusion. She cannot see Bottom for what he really is – half a man and half an ass. But if there are both sensuality and comedy here, there is also innocent delight. The dialogue between Bottom and his four little fairy servants is of the greatest charm. And we must recognize that charm is a crucial element in the play. But, above all, we must use our ears, eyes and imaginations. Much of the language in the scenes which present Bottom in Fairyland is of the greatest beauty, while the visual spectacle with which we are presented is superb. Finally, we must surrender our imaginations to all the rich possibilities that these scenes conjure up for us. We are in a world which is at once very real and totally illusory, at once most moving and very comic, at once highly sensuous and wholly innocent. These divided and complex feelings, all working together, suggest the true richness of the delight *A Midsummer Night's Dream* has to offer. Around the simple character of Bottom these emotions centre. One of the great ironies of the play is that this ham actor whose hopes of presenting a great tragedy to his noble master are in reality so laughable is, none the less, at the very heart of the most beautiful of all the illusions in Shakespeare's play. Although when he wakes from his dream Bottom can scarcely remember what has happened to him – and scarcely believe the few things he does remember – he is chosen to play a leading role in that most beautiful illusion where he spends the night with the Fairy Queen. The tragedy he hopes to perform may be a comic disaster, but Bottom is an actor in the greatest dramatic illusion of the play.

It is in another light, as 'Bully Bottom', the great ham actor, that we last see him. He has been released from the illusory world of Fairyland – a world of ease, beauty and enjoyment – and is now trying to create his own illusory world of the theatre. How engagingly inept is his performance as the tragic lover Pyramus! He rants and raves and over-acts – his suicide is one of the most ludicrous moments in English theatre   but while we laugh at him we should also be, as Theseus tells his courtiers, sympathetic towards the simple man's evident loyalty.

What happens to Bottom makes him a marvellously varied character. He joins together all three groups of characters in the play – the aristocrats, the fairies and the mechanicals - and he makes comments which are vital to the theme of illusion and reality (see pp. 81–6). He is on one hand a leading actor in the most beautiful illusion created by the fairies and, on the other hand, the leading actor in the absurd dramatic illusion that the mechanicals hope to create. Bottom is at once foolish and amusing but, above all, he is a character involved in a poetic beauty which he himself cannot entirely appreciate.

# Commentary



## LANGUAGE

The language of *A Midsummer Night's Dream* is rich and diverse. We have already seen (pp. 64–8) how important it is in the characterization of the young lovers. At one extreme, they are capable of uttering speeches of the greatest sophistication and refinement. Whenever they express their ardour – whether it is passion which they think they genuinely feel or new love kindled in them by the juice of Oberon's flower – their language is both beautiful and highly contrived. We may like to think here of the dialogue between Lysander and Hermia in the first scene of the play. However, for all its nobility of utterance, Shakespeare is determined that we should laugh at such high-flown feeling. We may be touched by the dialogue of Lysander and Hermia in the first scene, but we should compare it to that of Demetrius when he has had the magic juice poured on his eyes. When he wakes up, his new-found emotions for Helena are a complete illusion, but he thinks they are genuine enough, so he expresses himself with all the ardour and refinement that a young aristocrat in love should use (III, ii, 137–44). But we are no longer beguiled by the beauty of the words. We laugh at them. Demetrius's behaviour is quite absurd. The ornate language he speaks in is ridiculous.

We have also mentioned that there is another extreme of language used by the lovers. While they are capable of expressing what they think of as refined ardour, they can also use down-to-earth and even callous speech. The language with which the young men chide their women when they are no longer in love with them is blunt and hard. When Helena and Hermia row with each other, they also completely forget the refined tone that noble lovers should always use. This contrast, between the high-flown on the one hand and the ordinary and everyday on the other, is a crucial part of Shakespeare's comic effect.

Much of the most enduringly beautiful poetry in the play is spoken by the fairies. Indeed, it is largely through the power of such language that Shakespeare convinces us of the magical loveliness of Fairyland and the ethereal nature of Oberon, Titania and their followers. How does Shakespeare create this verbal magic? Let us look at the famous speech in which Oberon describes the bank where Titania sleeps after her revels (II, i, 249–67). Perhaps the first thing to notice is that although this passage is a description, it is very far from being a simple picture. It does more than merely describe a bank covered with flowers. Such a bank is, by its very nature, something beautiful, but Oberon's description derives much of its magic from its precision and its sense of real, lush vegetation. He lists six flowers that grow on the bank. These flowers are either sweet, simple and strongly coloured such as oxlips or violets, or they have richly evocative and sensuous names such as muskroses and eglantine. Notice too how the verbs that Oberon uses seem to make the whole bank pulse with life. The flowers do not simply grow here, they nod or blow or 'overcanopy'. The precision and variety with which Oberon so effortlessly expresses all of this help us to feel the very throb of nature beating through Titania's sleeping place. Our heightened sense of imagined life makes the bank appear magical. We know it is real, but the language makes the reality so intense that it seems to become part of the imaginative land of the fairies. It is the perfect setting for Titania. Notice how Oberon's language manages to convey the painless ease and rapture of such a world. Oberon describes Titania as lying on the bank and being 'lulled in these flowers with dances and delight'. Listen to how skilfully the 'l' sounds are used, and to how the richness of the vowels and the delicacy of the rhythm correspond exactly to a world which only such a fabulous creature as Titania could enjoy.

All the speeches of the fairies, whether they be ethereal creatures like Titania or mischievous spirits like Puck, are sharply detailed and imaginatively vivid. You may like to reread Puck's first description of himself (II, i, 42–57). The excitement he takes in physical pranks is exactly conveyed through the physical excitement of the language. By contrast, we should look at the speech of Titania in the same scene (ll.

121–37), where she is describing something of rapturous beauty. She tells how she sat with the mother of the little Indian boy beside the Indian Ocean and watched the great merchant ships crossing it. What she is picturing is by its very nature rare and exotic. Titania enhances our feelings of this by telling us that the air was 'spicèd', while her picture of the great merchant ships creates a sense of richness and power. The image of the Queen of the Fairies sitting on the yellow sand by an Indian princess and watching the swelling sails of the ships becomes a precise but very evocative vision. Then, Titania deftly compares the swelling sails of the ships to the swelling womb of the pregnant princess. The vision is so strong that we fully appreciate why Titania feels responsible for the little boy once his mother has died. Perhaps only Oberon's description of how the little flower came to have its powers of illusion (II, i, 155–69) surpasses Titania's ravishing vision.

The sense of wondrous beauty and natural power pulses through all the speeches of the fairies. It convinces us that they are at one with the forces of nature, that they are vividly and naturally alive, and that they are spirits who do indeed have power and influence in the natural world. But if the language of the fairies does often show their power and their oneness with nature, it can also express their kindliness towards humankind. At the end of the play, when Oberon and Puck have undone the confusion they have inflicted on the mortals and come to Theseus's palace to bless the marriages, their language becomes that of little benevolent sprites. No longer are they 'proud Titania' and 'jealous Oberon'; no longer do they speak in iambic pentameters, lines that have five stressed and five unstressed syllables. Their language now moves rapidly, with only seven syllables to the line, and is in couplets throughout. Indeed, their language moves with the lightness and speed with which the benevolent little spirits flit through the house of the mortals. It is the language of harmless and kindly little fairies, but it is still precise and at one with the forces of nature. Oberon is no longer the King of Fairyland listening to the ravishing sound of mermaids singing from dolphins' backs. He is a little household spirit come to wish natural joys on the far grander world of the newly married mortals.

Just as the worlds of the young lovers and the fairies have their special languages, so the world of the mechanicals comes alive for us through the language that they speak. Their medium is prose. But what marvellous prose it is! Though it has none of the fine phrases and magically evocative, natural details of the lovers and the fairies, the speech of Bottom when he wakes from the illusion (IV, i, 199–216) is extraordinarily powerful. The sense of bewilderment, the half-guessed-at magical experience – the convincing sensation of having woken from a rapturous dream – cannot fail to touch us. But if we are moved, we must, as always in this play, laugh as well. Though what Bottom has to express touches us, his confusion is also very funny. In his bewilderment, he talks of hearing eyes, seeing ears and tasting hands; his language reflects his own confusion. Furthermore, his resolution to have Peter Quince write a ballad – a simple countryman's poem – about the dream is again charming. After all, Bottom has just been beguiled by the most beautiful and sophisticated language and music. With what ease Shakespeare seems to end the speech when Bottom, fully awake now, resolves to sing the ballad of 'Bottom's Dream' before the Duke. The whole speech gives a brilliant impression of a very ordinary man waking from a rapturous dream, half remembering it – and then, as he becomes more awake, returning to the ordinary world of loyalty and duty which is truly his.

While the prose of the mechanicals is both comic and subtle, we should also appreciate the fun which Shakespeare takes in satirizing the worst excesses of poetry in their play-within-the-play. They have chosen a high and tragic subject, the story of Pyramus and Thisbe. The language which they lavish on the story is as absurd as the stage production which they hope to present. We could call the language of the play 'bombastic'. It tries to be grand but succeeds in being little more than noise and nonsense – as, for example, the ridiculous alliteration of the prologue (see p. 57). If we want to appreciate the full range of the language in *A Midsummer Night's Dream*, we might compare this woeful stuff to the effortless grace and imaginative variety in the speeches of the fairies. By contrast, the language in the play-within-the-play is language at its most flat and ridiculous. And yet the very absurdity and impoverishment of the poetry in the mechanicals' performance is an essential part of the range and richness of language in *A Midsummer Night's Dream* as a whole.

## ILLUSION AND REALITY

A play is an illusion. When we go to the theatre we know that we are going to see a performance by actors who are pretending to be the characters they portray rather than the people they actually are. The great pleasure which the theatre offers is this very illusion. In a sense, we know that we are being fooled. We know that what we are seeing is a world of make-believe. However, we willingly surrender to this illusion and thereby derive a great deal of pleasure from the theatre.

Perhaps no other English playwright was so conscious of this world of dramatic illusion as Shakespeare. Time and again in his comedies he plays with the idea of reality and illusion. First of all he creates for us in the audience the illusory world presented by his play. But very often he goes much further than this. He shows the characters in his play – illusory characters created by real actors – suffering from illusions. It is also often the case that, while these imaginary characters are suffering from illusions, they come to learn what is true or good about the real world which we suppose them to live in.

Nowhere is this more the case than in *A Midsummer Night's Dream*. All the characters are involved in illusions here. The young lovers, who believe that their quickly changing emotions are powerful and true, all meet up in the forest. Here the fairies squeeze the juice of a magic flower into the eyes of the male characters. Their emotions are no longer under control: they are illusions. The young men, who had believed themselves passionate and sincere when they were back in Athens, instantly fall out of love with the women who had once meant everything to them, and fall passionately for women they had previously rejected. They believe that their new feelings are wholly sincere. We can see that they are illusions. The comedy lies in the fact that *we* can tell the difference between illusion and reality, whereas those who are suffering from the power of Oberon's juice can not.

But the young lovers are not the only ones to undergo illusions. Titania, the Queen of the Fairies, is also the victim of an illusion. Because she refuses to surrender to Oberon the little Indian boy, he squeezes the juice of the magic flower on to her eyes and she falls passionately in love with the absurdly transformed figure of Bottom. The Fairy Queen lavishes on her new lover all the wealth, beauty and magic that her world of Fairyland has to provide. She too behaves sincerely, and yet appears absurd to us.

And Bottom is also involved in a world of illusion. Indeed, he is more deeply involved in such things than almost any of the other characters in *A Midsummer Night's Dream*. On the one hand he wants to create a deliberate illusion – the tragedy of *Pyramus and Thisbe* – while on the other hand he is the willing victim of the most beautiful illusion of the entire play, when, transformed into an ass, he becomes the beloved of the Fairy Queen and spends the night beside her.

If all three groups of characters in the play – the noble young lovers, the fairies and the mechanicals – are involved in illusion, so are we in the audience. We have come to the theatre with the deliberate intention of being beguiled by the dramatic illusion which the playwright and his actors offer us. For a couple of hours or so we sit in a real theatre but are transported into a world of the imagination. Our bodies are in one place, our minds and feelings are somewhere magically different. Like the young lovers, like Titania and Bottom, we are the victims of an illusion. Only at the end of the play, when one of the illusory dramatic characters who has so entertained us comes forward and asks us to applaud, is that world of dramatic illusion suddenly broken. In part, it is broken by us. Just as the characters in the play wake from the illusions which now appear to them as dreamlike, so we in the audience, as we loudly applaud the play we have just seen, shatter the illusion that has been created. We are no longer in the world of the imagination which we have so greatly enjoyed; like Bottom, Titania and the young lovers, we return to our true selves. We have been in Fairyland, the world of illusion. At the end of the play we are returned to the real and everyday world.

Perhaps the first point to appreciate about the clever way Shakespeare plays with the worlds of illusion and reality is our delight at being led so easily through all its complexities. The intricacies of the plot, the absurdity and reversals in which the characters are involved, are bewitching. Precisely because we surrender to the dramatic illusion that the play has to offer – because we believe while we are watching it that it is true – the juggling with confused and different worlds delights us. However, we should realize that this delight has its serious aspects. Nowhere is this more clear than in the presentation of the young lovers.

All four of them – and in particular the men – are involved in rapid and extreme changes of feeling. For example, while he was still in the 'real' world of Athens, Demetrius courted Helena, jilted her and fell in love with Hermia. In the wood, he falls in love with Helena once again, and jilts Hermia. In other words, he behaves with the same irresponsibility when he is a lover in the real world as he does when he is a lover in a magical and illusory world of the fairies. When Demetrius returns to the 'real' world of Athens at the end of the play, he is once more in love with Helena. To be sure, this is a happy ending. But none of the human characters in the play realizes that the love which Demetrius feels for Helena is not 'real'. In fact, it is a result of the illusion created by Oberon when he squeezed the juice of the flower into Demetrius's eyes. It is all very neat, very comic, and very delightful. But may it not be the case that Shakespeare is suggesting something serious here? What is love really like, if it is fickle in the 'real' world and equally fickle in the illusory world of the fairies' wood? What Shakespeare seems to be showing us is that love is of its very nature flighty and irresponsible. Those who fall victim to it fall victim to emotions which are blind, hasty and, in many ways, as childishly irresponsible as Cupid himself. Passionate love, whether it takes place in the 'real' world of Athens or in the magical world of the woods, is an emotion which makes people ardent and ridiculous. Wherever it is, love seems to bring with it illusions, confusions and changes.

The illusory world created by love can be painful and humiliating as well as enjoyable, as the character of Titania demonstrates. To gain his revenge, her husband contrives matters so that this regal and ethereally beautiful woman falls in love with a very ordinary man transformed into an ass. Just as the human lovers are often beguiled, so the Fairy Queen is tricked and humiliated through the illusions that love creates. On the other hand, just as the human lovers are ultimately led towards the mature world of married love, so the illusion inflicted on Titania becomes the means by which Oberon obtains from her the little Indian boy whom she has previously refused to grant him. Their married happiness is restored, and happiness and harmony return to nature.

Finally, we should look in some detail at the last act. The play itself opens in the 'real' world of Athens and then moves into the world of magic and illusion contained in the wood. In the same way, at its close, we come out of that world and return to the 'real' world of Athens. All the lovers are harmoniously reunited in the mature world of marriage. Bottom has been freed from his magic dream and now tries to create the illusory world of his play for the amusement of the courtiers. However, the young lovers cannot always distinguish between illusion and reality, and so get themselves involved in amusing confusions, and similarly Bottom, the would-be great actor, cannot understand that the drama is an illusion and that reality has no place within it. He gets confused between the illusory world created by a play and the real world of everyday experience. Partly as a result of these absurd confusions – though we should note that they are no more absurd than the confusions of the lovers in the wood – his play is a disastrous but comical failure. The illusions which it must create, in order to have any success, evaporate before the very audience which wants them to succeed. None the less, as Theseus points out, though the mechanicals' play fails completely on the level of an illusion, it succeeds on a far more important level. It proves to the Duke that the real working men of Athens are truly devoted to him. The real emotions that prompt them to create this illusion are honest and worthy.

*A Midsummer Night's Dream* does not end with this world of newly mature and harmonious lovers and simple men who have escaped from the illusions of the woods. How dull it would be if, after so much delight, we should be returned merely to the 'real' world. The play ends with the most beautiful of illusions – the world of Fairyland. The fairies, who have created so much of the confusion in the play, return to bring order, harmony and blessings. His audience may or may not have believed in fairies, but when Shakespeare's own creations appear on the stage, we are all beguiled. The world of magic and imagination which has been so important is reconciled with the 'real' world of the newly married lovers in Athens. The bringers of illusion are united in love and concord with the 'real' world of human beings. This is a beautiful final dramatic illusion.

And, at the end of the play, it is broken. Puck steps forward. He is no longer simply Oberon's servant. He exists now in a curious half-world – a world half of illusion and half of reality – in which he is at one and the same time Puck himself and the actor creating the illusory character of Puck, who steps forward now and asks us to break the dramatic illusion by bidding us applaud, so that we wake from the dream which we have so greatly enjoyed.

# *Examination Questions*

1. Read the following passage carefully and answer the questions
beneath it.


OBERON  How long within this wood intend you stay?                              1
TITANIA  Perchance till after Theseus' wedding day.
    If you will patiently dance in our round
    And see our moonlight revels, go with us.
    If not, shun me, and I will spare your haunts.                              5
OBERON  Give me that boy and I will go with thee.
TITANIA  Not for thy fairy kingdom! Fairies, away.
    We shall chide downright if I longer stay.

*Exit Titania with her train*

OBERON  Well, go thy way. Thou shalt not from this grove
    Till I torment thee for this injury.                                        10
    My gentle Puck, come hither. Thou rememberest
    Since once I sat upon a promontory,
    And heard a mermaid on a dolphin's back
    Uttering such dulcet and harmonious breath
    That the rude sea grew civil at her song,                                   15
    And certain stars shot madly from their spheres
    To hear the sea-maid's music?
PUCK                              I remember.
OBERON  That very time I saw – but thou couldst not –
    Flying between the cold moon and the earth
    Cupid, all armed. A certain aim he took                                     20
    At a fair vestal thronèd by the west,
    And loosed his loveshaft smartly from his bow
    As it should pierce a hundred thousand hearts;
    But I might see young Cupid's fiery shaft
    Quenched in the chaste beams of the watery moon,                            25
    And the imperial votaress passed on

In maiden meditation, fancy-free.
Yet marked I where the bolt of Cupid fell:
It fell upon a little western flower,
Before, milk-white; now purple with love's wound:                30
And maidens call it 'love in idleness'.
Fetch me that flower – the herb I showed thee once.

(i)  Explain, briefly, the situation at this point in the play.

(ii)  Put into modern English lines 11–16 (from *Thou rememberest ...* to *... their spheres*).

(iii)  Explain the reference to *Cupid, all armed* (line 20).

(iv)  Comment, briefly, on the use Shakespeare makes of poetic language in this passage.

(v)  Why does Oberon send Puck to fetch the flower 'love in idleness'?

(vi)  What does this passage tell us about the behaviour and outlook of the fairies?

*(Oxford and Cambridge Schools Examination Board, 1982)*

2. BOTTOM  ... Methought I was – and methought I had – but man is but a patched fool if he will offer to say what methought I had. The eye of man hath not heard, the ear of man hath not seen, man's hand is not able to taste, his tongue to conceive, nor his heart to report what my dream was!

(i)  What are Bottom's *first* thoughts when he awakens?
(ii)  Explain 'but man is but a patched fool ... methought I had.'
(iii)  What is amusing in Bottom's language here? Where else in the play do his words produce a similar effect?

*(Southern Universities Joint Board, 1979)*

3. DEMETRIUS (*wakes*)   O Helen, goddess, nymph, perfect, divine –
To what, my love, shall I compare thine eyne?
Crystal is muddy! O, how ripe in show
Thy lips – those kissing cherries – tempting grow!
That pure congealed white, high Taurus' snow,
Fanned with the eastern wind, turns to a crow

When thou holdest up thy hand. O, let me kiss
This princess of pure white, this seal of bliss!
HELENA   O spite! O hell! I see you all are bent
To set against me for your merriment.


(i)  Why does Demetrius utter these words? *Briefly*, explain Helena's reaction to this speech.

(ii)  Point out three different features of the language and style of Demetrius's speech.

(iii)  Why does Helena feel insulted? *Briefly*, explain how the confusion is eventually settled amicably.

(*Southern Universities Joint Board, 1980*)


4.  OBERON   ... A certain aim he took
At a fair vestal thronèd by the west,
And loosed his loveshaft smartly from his bow
As it should pierce a hundred thousand hearts;
But I might see young Cupid's fiery shaft
Quenched in the chaste beams of the watery moon,
And the imperial votaress passed on
In maiden meditation, fancy-free.
Yet marked I where the bolt of Cupid fell:
It fell upon a little western flower,


(i)  Briefly relate, in your own words, the story Oberon tells here.

(ii)  Explain the meaning of lines 7–8 ('And the imperial votaress . . . fancy-free.')

(iii)  What is the importance of this story to the subsequent course of the play? What other purpose was the story intended to serve when Shakespeare wrote it?

(*Southern Universities Joint Board, 1981*)


5.  TITANIA   The ox hath therefore stretched his yoke in vain,
The ploughman lost his sweat, and the green corn
Hath rotted ere his youth attained a beard.
The fold stands empty in the drownèd field,

And crows are fatted with the murrion flock.
The nine men's morris is filled up with mud,
And the quaint mazes in the wanton green
For lack of tread are undistinguishable.

(i)  How do the contents of the speech suggest the setting and action of the play?

(ii)  Explain clearly lines 6–8 ('The nine men's ... undistinguishable').

(iii)  What is the basic cause of the events described in this speech? How sympathetic to Titania are you, both at the beginning and later in the play?

(*Southern Universities Joint Board, 1982*)

6. THESEUS   Now is the mural down between the two neighbours.
DEMETRIUS   No remedy, my lord, when walls are so wilful to hear without warning.
HIPPOLYTA   This is the silliest stuff that ever I heard.
THESEUS   The best in this kind are but shadows; and the worst are no worse, if imagination amend them.
HIPPOLYTA   It must be your imagination, then, and not theirs.
THESEUS   If we imagine no worse of them than they of themselves, they may pass for excellent men. Here come two noble beasts in, a man and a lion.

(i)  Indicate in a few words what different attitudes among the courtiers may be discerned in the comments above.

(ii)  What is meant by 'the best in this kind are but shadows'? What attitude to actors and the theatre do you think these words may be intended to convey?

(iii)  How does this extract contribute to the comedy of the scene? Can we both laugh at, and sympathize with, the workmen in their play-acting?

(*Southern Universities Joint Board, 1982*)

7.  'The play seems to set out to make fun of love and lovers.' Do you agree with this comment on *A Midsummer Night's Dream*?

(*Southern Universities Joint Board, 1979*)

8. What do the 'rude mechanicals' contribute to *A Midsummer Night's Dream?*

*(Southern Universities Joint Board, 1980)*


9. '*A Midsummer Night's Dream* abounds in humour, both in words and in situations.' Illustrate and discuss the effectiveness of the various kinds of humour in the play.

*(Southern Universities Joint Board, 1981)*


10. 'Oberon is a powerful and selfish character.' Discuss this view and indicate his importance in the play.

*(Southern Universities Joint Board, 1982)*


11. 'The courtiers are just as silly as the mechanicals, but they are neither so kind nor so amusing.' What do you think?

*(Oxford and Cambridge Schools Examination Board, 1982)*


12. 'When faced with fairies or clever courtiers, Bottom triumphs by plain common sense.' What is your view?

*(Oxford and Cambridge Schools Examination Board, 1982)*


13. 'In *A Midsummer Night's Dream* love is a form of madness.' Discuss.

*(Oxford and Cambridge Schools Examination Boad, 1982)*

# MORE ABOUT PENGUINS, PELICANS
# AND PUFFINS

For further information about books available from Penguins please write to Dept EP, Penguin Books Ltd, Harmondsworth, Middlesex UB7 0DA.

*In the U.S.A.*: For a complete list of books available from Penguins in the United States write to Dept DG, Penguin Books, 299 Murray Hill Parkway, East Rutherford, New Jersey 07073.

*In Canada*: For a complete list of books available from Penguins in Canada write to Penguin Books Canada Ltd, 2801 John Street, Markham, Ontario L3R 1B4.

*In Australia*: For a complete list of books available from Penguins in Australia write to the Marketing Department, Penguin Books Australia Ltd, P.O. Box 257, Ringwood, Victoria 3134.

*In New Zealand*: For a complete list of books available from Penguins in New Zealand write to the Marketing Department, Penguin Books (N.Z.) Ltd, Private Bag, Takapuna, Auckland 9.

*In India*: For a complete list of books available from Penguins in India write to Penguin Overseas Ltd, 706 Eros Apartments, 56 Nehru Place, New Delhi 110019.

# PLAYS IN PENGUINS

□ **Edward Albee** *Who's Afraid of Virginia Woolf?* £1.75
□ **Alan Ayckbourn** *The Norman Conquests* £2.95
□ **Bertolt Brecht** *Parables for the Theatre (The Good Woman of Setzuan/The Caucasian Chalk Circle)* £1.95
□ **Anton Chekhov** *Plays (The Cherry Orchard/The Three Sisters/Ivanov/The Seagull/Uncle Vania)* £2.50
□ **Henrik Ibsen** *Hedda Gabler/Pillars of Society/The Wild Duck* £2.50
□ **Eugène Ionesco** *Absurd Drama (The Rhinoceros/The Chair/The Lesson)* £3.50
□ **Ben Jonson** *Three Comedies (Volpone/The Alchemist/Bartholomew Fair)* £2.95
□ **D. H. Lawrence** *Three Plays (The Collier's Friday Night/The Daughter-in-Law/The Widowing of Mrs Holroyd)* £2.95
□ **Arthur Miller** *Death of a Salesman* £1.50
□ **John Mortimer** *A Voyage Round My Father/What Shall We Tell Caroline?/The Dock Brief* £3.50
□ **J. B. Priestley** *Time and the Conways/I Have Been Here Before/The Inspector Calls/The Linden Tree* £2.95
□ **Peter Shaffer** *Amadeus* £2.50
□ **Bernard Shaw** *Plays Pleasant (Arms and the Man/Candida/The Man of Destiny/You Never Can Tell)* £2.25
□ **Sophocles** *Three Theban Plays (Oedipus the King/Antigone/Oedipus at Colonus)* £2.95
□ **Arnold Wesker** *The Wesker Trilogy (Chicken Soup with Barley/Roots/I'm Talking about Jerusalem)* £2.95
□ **Oscar Wilde** *Plays (Lady Windermere's Fan/A Woman of No Importance/An Ideal Husband/The Importance of Being Earnest/Salomé)* £1.95
□ **Thornton Wilder** *Our Town/The Skin of Our Teeth/The Matchmaker* £1.95
□ **Tennessee Williams** *Sweet Bird of Youth/A Streetcar Named Desire/The Glass Menagerie* £2.50

# PENGUIN BOOKS OF POETRY

| | | |
|---|---|---|
| ☐ | *American Verse* | £5.95 |
| ☐ | *Ballads* | £2.95 |
| ☐ | *British Poetry Since 1945* | £4.95 |
| ☐ | *A Choice of Comic and Curious Verse* | £4.50 |
| ☐ | *Contemporary American Poetry* | £2.95 |
| ☐ | *Contemporary British Poetry* | £2.50 |
| ☐ | *Eighteenth-Century Verse* | £3.95 |
| ☐ | *Elizabethan Verse* | £3.95 |
| ☐ | *English Poetry 1918–60* | £2.95 |
| ☐ | *English Romantic Verse* | £3.95 |
| ☐ | *English Verse* | £2.95 |
| ☐ | *First World War Poetry* | £2.50 |
| ☐ | *Georgian Poetry* | £2.50 |
| ☐ | *Irish Verse* | £3.50 |
| ☐ | *Light Verse* | £5.95 |
| ☐ | *London in Verse* | £2.95 |
| ☐ | *Love Poetry* | £3.95 |
| ☐ | *The Metaphysical Poets* | £2.95 |
| ☐ | *Modern African Poetry* | £3.95 |
| ☐ | *New Poetry* | £2.95 |
| ☐ | *Poems of Science* | £4.95 |
| ☐ | *Poetry of the Thirties* | £2.95 |
| ☐ | *Post-War Russian Poetry* | £2.50 |
| ☐ | *Spanish Civil War Verse* | £4.50 |
| ☐ | *Unrespectable Verse* | £3.50 |
| ☐ | *Victorian Verse* | £3.50 |
| ☐ | *Women Poets* | £3.95 |

# ENGLISH AND AMERICAN LITERATURE IN PENGUINS

☐ ***Emma*** Jane Austen £1.25

'I am going to take a heroine whom no one but myself will much like,' declared Jane Austen of Emma, her most spirited and controversial heroine in a comedy of self-deceit and self-discovery.

☐ ***Tender is the Night*** F. Scott Fitzgerald £2.95

Fitzgerald worked on seventeen different versions of this novel, and its obsessions – idealism, beauty, dissipation, alcohol and insanity – were those that consumed his own marriage and his life.

☐ ***The Life of Johnson*** James Boswell £2.95

Full of gusto, imagination, conversation and wit, Boswell's immortal portrait of Johnson is as near a novel as a true biography can be, and still regarded by many as the finest 'life' ever written. This shortened version is based on the 1799 edition.

☐ ***A House and its Head*** Ivy Compton-Burnett £4.95

In a novel 'as trim and tidy as a hand-grenade' (as Pamela Hansford Johnson put it), Ivy Compton-Burnett penetrates the facade of a conventional, upper-class Victorian family to uncover a chasm of violent emotions – jealousy, pain, frustration and sexual passion.

☐ ***The Trumpet Major*** Thomas Hardy £1.50

Although a vein of unhappy unrequited love runs through this novel, Hardy also draws on his warmest sense of humour to portray Wessex village life at the time of the Napoleonic wars.

☐ ***The Complete Poems of Hugh MacDiarmid***

☐ Volume One £8.95
☐ Volume Two £8.95

The definitive edition of work by the greatest Scottish poet since Robert Burns, edited by his son Michael Grieve, and W. R. Aitken.

# ENGLISH AND AMERICAN LITERATURE IN PENGUINS

☐ ***Main Street*** **Sinclair Lewis** £4.95

The novel that added an immortal chapter to the literature of America's Mid-West, *Main Street* contains the comic essence of Main Streets everywhere.

☐ ***The Compleat Angler*** **Izaak Walton** £2.50

A celebration of the countryside, and the superiority of those in 1653, as now, who love *quietnesse, vertue* and, above all, *Angling*. 'No fish, however coarse, could wish for a doughtier champion than Izaak Walton' – Lord Home

☐ ***The Portrait of a Lady*** **Henry James** £2.50

'One of the two most brilliant novels in the language', according to F. R. Leavis, James's masterpiece tells the story of a young American heiress, prey to fortune-hunters but not without a will of her own.

☐ ***Hangover Square*** **Patrick Hamilton** £3.95

Part love story, part thriller, and set in the publands of London's Earls Court, this novel caught the conversational tone of a whole generation in the uneasy months before the Second World War.

☐ ***The Rainbow*** **D. H. Lawrence** £2.50

Written between *Sons and Lovers* and *Women in Love*, *The Rainbow* covers three generations of Brangwens, a yeoman family living on the borders of Nottinghamshire.

☐ ***Vindication of the Rights of Woman***
**Mary Wollstonecraft** £2.95

Although Walpole once called her 'a hyena in petticoats', Mary Wollstonecraft's vision was such that modern feminists continue to go back and debate the arguments so powerfully set down here.

# ENGLISH AND AMERICAN LITERATURE IN PENGUINS

☐ *Nostromo* **Joseph Conrad**                              £1.95

In his most ambitious and successful novel Conrad created an entire imaginary republic in South America. As he said, 'you shall find there according to your deserts: encouragement, consolation, fear, charm – all you demand – and, perhaps, also that glimpse of truth for which you forgot to ask.'

☐ *A Passage to India* **E. M. Forster**                    £2.50

Centred on the unsolved mystery at the Marabar Caves, Forster's masterpiece conveys, as no other novel has done, the troubled spirit of India during the Raj.

---

These books should be available at all good bookshops or news-agents, but if you live in the UK or the Republic of Ireland and have difficulty in getting to a bookshop, they can be ordered by post. Please indicate the titles required and fill in the form below.

NAME _________________________________________________ BLOCK CAPITALS

ADDRESS _____________________________________________________________

_____________________________________________________________________

---

Enclose a cheque or postal order payable to The Penguin Bookshop to cover the total price of books ordered, plus 50p for postage. Readers in the Republic of Ireland should send £IR equivalent to the sterling prices, plus 67p for postage. Send to: The Penguin Bookshop, 54/56 Bridlesmith Gate, Nottingham, NG1 2GP.

You can also order by phoning (0602) 599295, and quoting your Barclaycard or Access number.

Every effort is made to ensure the accuracy of the price and availability of books at the time of going to press, but it is sometimes necessary to increase prices and in these circumstances retail prices may be shown on the covers of books which may differ from the prices shown in this list or elsewhere. This list is not an offer to supply any book.

**This order service is only available to residents in the UK and the Republic of Ireland.**